# SPALDING®

# SOCCER STRATEGIES

## Jerry Yeagley

MASTERS PRESS

*A Subsidiary of Howard W. Sams & Co.*

Published by Masters Press (a subsidiary of Howard W. Sams)
2647 Waterfront Pkwy E. Dr, Suite 300, Indianapolis, IN 46214

**Library of Congress Cataloging-in-Publication Data**
Yeagley, Jerry.

     Spalding soccer strategies / Jerry Yeagley.
         p.   cm. – (Spalding sports library. Soccer ; 4)
     ISBN 0-940279-49-5 : $9.95

     1. Soccer--Coaching. I. Title. II. Series.

GV943.8.Y43   1992                     92-17823
796.334'07'7--dc20                      CIP

*Cover photograph by Kent Phillips. All inside photographs by Kent Phillips except on page viii, which was provided by the Sports Information Department at Indiana University.*

*Fitness illustrations by Rita Powell.*

*To Barney Hoffman, my high school coach, and Mel Lorback, my college coach — men who taught me about life as well as soccer.*

and

*To Bill Armstrong, whose friendship and unyielding support helped make Indiana soccer what it is today.*

# Acknowledgments

To Mark Montieth, for editing the manuscript.

To Yvette Yeagley and David Tanner, for helping to prepare the manuscript.

To assistant coaches Joe Kelley and Don Rawson, for their guidance and assistance.

To John Schrader, trainer, and Frank Eksten, strength coach, for their contributions.

# Contents

# Preface

In 1963, soccer was barely a rumor at Indiana University. A club team had been allowed to participate for several years, but it was no more than a recreational outlet for interested students. The university provided little funding, and offered no scholarships.

Today, Indiana has perhaps the best collegiate program in the nation. It has won three NCAA championships, has competed in the Final Four nine times and plays in its own state-of-the-art stadium.

What happened in the meantime?

Jerry Yeagley.

No college team in the United States bears the imprint of one person as much as Indiana's soccer team does. After taking over as coach of the club team in 1963, Yeagley fought for 10 years to have it elevated to a varsity sport. Once that battle was won, he wasted no time turning it into one of the elite programs in the country. By 1976, the Hoosiers were competing for the national championship. In 1982, they won the first of their three titles. Throughout the 1980s they won more games and had the best winning percentage (.813) of any team in the nation. They remain a national power today.

If that sounds like a Cinderella story it's nothing new for Yeagley, who's been handy with a glass slipper throughout his soccer career. Back in tiny Myerstown, Pa, where he was one of just 47 kids in his high school graduating class, Yeagley helped lead his team to the state championship, upsetting a much larger school in the final game. At West Chester State, a small Pennsylvania college, he helped lead his team to the NCAA Division I championship in 1961, upsetting heavily-favored St. Louis University in the final game.

After completing work on his Master's Degree at the University of Pittsburgh in 1963, Yeagley was ready for new challenges. He had offers to take over established programs in the East, but he spotted another Cinderella-in-waiting in Bloomington, Ind. Indiana University was no Myerstown High School or West Chester State as far as its size, but its soccer program was as humble as it could be. Build a soccer power in the heart of Big Ten football country? To Yeagley's way of thinking, it seemed like "a neat thing to do."

Yeagley's primary job at Indiana was to teach physical education. Supervising the soccer club was almost an afterthought. Technically, he wasn't even classified as a coach.

Yeagley experienced a culture shock when he arrived at Indiana. Soccer was virtually unknown to most sports fans in the Midwest then. Most sporting goods stores didn't even sell soccer balls. Few high schools fielded teams. At Yeagley's first call-out for practice at I.U., eight players showed up, and most of them were interested in knowing what trips the team would be taking so they could plan their parties accordingly. Yeagley remembers telling a woman at a restaurant during one of Indiana's early road trips that the group of young men before her were a soccer team. "Oh, soccer!" she said. "That's the game you play on horses, isn't it?"

Amid that environment of apathy and ignorance, Yeagley built his program from scratch. He grabbed the equipment the varsity sports were discarding. His players hung sheets on campus to publicize the games. As a group they lined the field, administered first aid to each other and drove to the road games in their own cars, stopping at the homes of parents for meals along the way — anything to save a few pennies.

Gradually, a program began to take shape. Competing against club teams and what few varsity programs existed in the Midwest then, Yeagley's teams won immediately. His first team went 5-1-3. The second finished 8-1-1. The third 9-1. Still, the university's administration at the time showed little interest in what was happening. In fact, Yeagley was told he was wasting his time trying to gain varsity status for an oddball sport such as soccer, and was encouraged to take a job elsewhere.

But he stayed. And won. In 1973, amid growing pressure from a few influential members of the student body, community and university administration, soccer was granted varsity status. Although he had no scholarships at first, Yeagley at least had more funding and the blessings of the athletic department. Finally armed with a launching pad, he fueled the takeoff.

His teams still soar today. In 19 years of varsity competition under Yeagley, the Hoosiers have won 328 games while losing just 57 and tying 27. They have competed in the NCAA tournament all but three of those years. Each one of his recruiting classes has competed for the national championship at least once.

Amid the team success, the individual honors have been many. Indiana has had 22 All-Americans, four Olympians, 36 professionals, 14 national team players, three national collegiate Players of the Year and two World Cup players. More than 20 of Yeagley's former players and assistants have become college coaches.

Yeagley too is well-decorated. He is the only person to be named Division I Coach of the Year twice. He has been inducted into the Pennsylvania Athletic Hall of Fame. And, in 1989, he received the highest honor of all: induction into the National Soccer Hall of Fame.

Indiana's soccer program has come a long way — from outcasts to champions. Another coach at Indiana who has won three national championships, Bob Knight, has recognized Yeagley's rare accomplishment.

"There are a lot of good coaches who have been able to develop good programs in various sports where there is a foundation for that particular sport," Knight said. "However, very, very few have been able to create something where there is no foundation.

"There is no valid reason why Indiana should have a great soccer team, yet Jerry has created a team that is nationally competitive and has been able to build a tradition where before there was absolutely none. What he has done is a unique and singular accomplishment for him as a coach. As I study college sports, I don't believe anyone, in any sport, at any school, has done what he has done with the soccer program here."

Throughout all the victories and all the honors, Yeagley hasn't lost sight of the reasons for his success. He realizes that the same fundamental strategies that enabled his early teams to win are just as important today as they were in 1963. This book relates those tactics, along with his unique coaching philosophies and approach to fitness.

THE EDITORS

 **1**

# Coaching
# Philosophies

**I** was fortunate during my playing days to be associated with two great coaches, men who taught me many important lessons about soccer and about people.

Barney Hoffman, my coach at Myerstown (Pa.) High School, not only taught me the basic skills of the game, he also helped me develop a love for it, to appreciate it. While playing for him, I decided I wanted to coach someday, even though my parents wanted me to become a dentist. Mel Lorback, my coach at West Chester State College, was a master psychologist and a great motivator as well as a superb tactician.

I played on championship teams for both of them, teams representing small schools that overcame the odds and defeated much larger schools. From these two coaches, I "learned how to win." That's a cliché, but there's something to it. I suppose lessons can be learned from losing, but lessons can be learned from winning as well. Winners learn what must be done to win and develop the confidence needed to do what it takes in pressure situations. They develop an attitude that doesn't allow them to settle for anything but their best.

If an athlete grows accustomed to losing, it's easy for him to convince himself that winning really doesn't matter. It does. A victory isn't worth cheating for, but it's certainly worth devoting 100 percent of one's effort toward. When I recruit, I look for student athletes who share that attitude. Ability obviously is important, but I want someone who knows how to win and expects to win.

Of course it's impossible for everyone to come from a championship program. Everyone has to learn how to win somewhere, and that's a coach's primary responsibility: developing a winning atmosphere. That doesn't necessarily mean winning a championship every year. A program can be successful without ever winning a championship, if the game is approached with the proper diligence and attitude.

That's one of the things I've learned through coaching over the years. I wasn't a very good loser when I first started. I let the losses really get to me, and I was very hard on myself. I still wouldn't classify myself as a *good* loser, but I do cope with disappointment much better.

I've learned to focus on the effort and performance in a game rather than merely the score. Early on I sometimes lost sight of those values. I have coached many victories in which the performance level wasn't up to the standard that it needed to be. And I have coached some losses in which our effort and performance levels were quite good. As coaches and players mature, they have to realize that the score is not always a true indicator of performance.

• • •

Coaches approach their relationship with their players in different ways. Some make it a point to keep a distance, to create a more businesslike relationship. They don't believe they can maintain proper control over the team if they are too friendly with their players.

That works for some coaches, but a lot of the enjoyment of coaching for me comes from developing close relationships with the players. I want to have their respect, but I also want to be their friend. I don't feel comfortable having a barrier there. I want to be integrated with them; that's the atmosphere in which I feel most comfortable.

Coaches have a great opportunity to influence a young person's behavior. I spent 16 years in the classroom at Indiana University as a physical education teacher. I enjoyed the classroom, but I believe through coaching

I have a greater chance of influencing the young people with whom I come in contact. Coaching to me is a higher form of teaching. I can get to know each player and what makes him tick; get to know his girlfriend, his parents, his problems and so on.

Coaches have a wonderful opportunity to affect how young people think and how they act, even how successful they'll be in life beyond their college years. It's a tremendous responsibility. I feel I can have a more positive influence on my players and do a better job as a coach by being involved with them rather than keeping a distance.

Getting close to the players also helps me maintain a youthful outlook. It's enjoyable working with college students. It keeps me up to date on things — although I have to admit the music I have to listen to in the locker room isn't as enjoyable as it used to be. But I still like fooling around with the guys. I still arm wrestle with them, and I'm not afraid to joke with them.

Of course a coach's approach for the most part must depend on his personality and what works best for him. Some coaches aren't comfortable with informality, but it works for me. I believe players want to respond positively to the coach and please him. They should want to perform their best for themselves and their teammates, but the coach fits in there somewhere. If athletes are playing in spite of the coach, or playing *to* spite the coach — an "I'll show you" kind of thing — that can be counterproductive.

Coaches have to keep in mind, however, that they can't have positive vibrations with everyone. Some personalities just don't mesh. But that doesn't mean players they don't feel particularly close to can't be successful members of the team.

Coaches who take the approach I do have to be particularly careful to maintain proper discipline. A close relationship with the players doesn't have to mean letting them do whatever they want to do. We have policies for the team. They're printed out and given to the players and their parents. We don't have a lot of rules, but we expect them to be followed. They include the obvious things about drinking and drugs, treating their teammates and other students with respect, going to class, and so on. They're expected to use good judgement and common sense. And there will be times the coach has to put the hammer down and use discipline.

Coaches need to identify the players on their teams who display the proper leadership qualities, and then make sure that leadership is exercised. I believe a coach can do this more effectively if he spends casual time with his players. In a relaxed setting, he gets to know them better and see who among them is most admired. If a coach distances himself from the players, he isn't likely to learn who the real leaders are.

By allowing the leadership on a team to come forth naturally, a coach reduces many potential discipline problems. A coach can't keep everyone in line by himself — he's outnumbered, and he can't be with the players all of the time. Players are going to challenge the rules to see what they can get away with. Someone on the team must be willing to step forward and say, "Hey, if you screw up you have to answer to me," to teammates who might go too far. The players must take pride in the team by assuming responsibility for each other.

The most difficult discipline problem I've had at Indiana occurred when I had to release some players from the team. We were having poor leadership; the leaders were leading in the wrong direction. This happened during the spring, in the off-season. Finally the internal discipline came forward and the young players came to the coaches and said, "We don't like this, and we want you to know what's going on."

The coaches had sensed something was wrong, but we weren't completely aware of the situation. We might not have figured it out if some of the players hadn't felt comfortable enough to approach us with the problem. As a result, five players were suspended and three of them were not allowed to return to the team the following season.

It's a bit scary to drop good players like that, but in the long run it paid off. We missed the talent of the players who had been dropped, but as a result the team had better unity. If we had allowed those players to remain on the team strictly because of their talent, it could have proved disastrous, due to the fragmented nature of the team at that time.

We reached the No. 1 ranking in the country the next year, and went from an underachieving team to an overachieving team. The discipline and attitude of the players always carries over to the field. No matter how much talent a coach has, if the discipline and attitude are wrong, he and the team aren't likely to be successful.

If a coach doesn't have a close relationship with his players, he isn't likely to detect the team's possible internal problems. It frightens me to think what might have happened to the team if those younger players hadn't felt comfortable enough to come forward and talk about the poor leadership they were getting. If a coach makes it a point to distance himself from his players, he runs the risk of never being aware of the atmosphere among the team.

I've also had to suspend players from games over the years, although not very often. Perhaps a player didn't go to class, skipped study table, or didn't meet with his tutor. In a college program, academics must be the top priority. The players must realize their first obligation is to their education.

The emphasis on academics should occur at every college, as well as at younger levels. Even on youth teams, the coach should take an interest in the players' academic progress. Soccer, and any sport, can be a great means of motivating players in the classroom. If a kid knows that he's likely to have to sit out a game or two, or perhaps lose his place on the team if he doesn't put forth an honest effort in the classroom, he'll probably take a more serious interest in his academics.

• • •

One of the primary strategic decisions a coach must make is what "formation" to employ. Over the years, a dizzying variety of systems have been used — 4-2-4, 4-3-3, 4-4-2, 3-5-2 . . . you name it, it's probably been tried.

When I played in high school and college, and when I began coaching, the W-M formation was the most common system of play. Coaches tend to use what was successful when they played, and that was what most teams were playing at the time.

Today it is common to have three or four players in the back, with a deep sweeper or an advanced one. Most teams have two primary markers, maybe a third if the other team has a third forward. We're also seeing more players in midfield now, providing width to the offense. In attack, teams can play with one, two or three front runners, each with a specific role.

I'm not much for numbers, however. The fact is, the formation isn't nearly as important as the roles that are assigned to the players. When someone asks me what system I use, I just smile. From one year to the next it could be completely different. It also can be different from one game to the next, depending on the opponent and on our personnel.

Early in my coaching career we tried some things that were uncommon at the time, such as playing four in the midfield. In those days, before the program had become established, we had to make a lot of adjustments because we had such a diverse range of talent within the team. We had some players whose skills were excellent, as well as inexperienced players with technical and tactical deficiencies. This is bound to be the case for many teams below the major college level.

Having such varied talent forced me to be creative in determining roles that enabled the players to become more successful individually and helped the team become more successful as a unit. We played a variety of systems from year to year, depending on our individual talent, how we wanted to use our better players and how we wanted to hide the players who were just learning the game. That was a great training ground for me as a coach.

For example, I had one player, Karl Schmidt, who was an all-American in 1967. He would be a striker one game, the sweeper the next game and play in the midfield in the next. It all depended on our opponent.

I believe determining roles for the players is crucial to successful coaching. There are no secrets with the X's and the O's in soccer. We all know the same principles of play. What is most important is finding the proper blend for the talent.

Ultimately, the proper blend is to have an entire team of players who can play anywhere on the field, players who — aside from the goalkeeper — are completely interchangeable. Such a system places few restrictions on the players; it's free-flowing and somewhat ad-libbed, and places constant pressure on the defense. As a result, it's the most difficult to defend.

Holland, with its "Clockwork Orange" attack in the 1970s, came closer than anyone to mastering this approach. A few of our teams came reasonably close, such as the one in the early 1980s that won two national championships. We really confused and frustrated defenses who were accustomed to seeing players in the same positions on the field throughout the game.

However, an offense must have purpose. The players can't be running helter-skelter around the field, moving just for the sake of moving. The primary factor in deciding how a team plays, both offensively and defensively, should be determined by the capabilities of the personnel.

A coach obviously wouldn't ask a player who's a good defender but has poor attacking skills to go forward with the ball very often. A coach must determine the capabilities of his players and ask them to play within them. Sometimes coaches expect players to do things that they aren't capable of doing. To ask players to do things they have trouble doing not only hinders their performance, it can be psychologically damaging for them and for their teammates.

For example, in 1991 we had five or six freshmen who played a great deal. We had a difficult time early in the season determining where they fit best. We kept things simple early on. We used the KISS principle — "keep it simple, stupid." We were quite predictable for our opponents, but at least we weren't confusing ourselves. We started out the season playing with three front runners, three in midfield and four in the back with a deep sweeper.

As our players developed and we learned more about what they could do, we changed our system of play. We used one advanced striker, a forward who played underneath the striker, an advanced central midfielder, a defensive central midfielder and two players who played wide at midfield.

The way we played in our first game was completely different than how we played in the finals of the NCAA tournament. That was an unusual year because we had so many young players, but coaches must be flexible at all times. It's often a mistake to lock into a formation at the start of the year and stick with it.

Coaches of more experienced teams usually can afford to be more consistent in their approach, although they still should be willing to make changes if it improves the team. Players might improve, or possibly take a step backward during the season, and a coach should make changes to accommodate the fluctuations in performance.

I don't recommend that coaches adopt a system and say, "This year I'm going to play a 3-5-2." Some people today, for example, say, "You've got to play five in the midfield, that's the modern game." But there's no magic in the numbers. A formation does not win a championship, players do.

The successful coaches are those who are able to mold their players into a cohesive unit by figuring out how they best complement each other. If five different coaches could take the same 11 players and work with them in setting up a team, the one who could achieve the best chemistry — such as by identifying the leaders and workhorses, hiding the weaker players and taking full advantage of each individual's skills — would be the most successful. That's where a coach's sixth sense is important.

I always admired Harry Keough, the coach at St. Louis University, during my early years of coaching. I felt he had that knack of being able to put 11 players on the field and get the best out of them as individuals and as a team. I've also seen coaches who made me wonder, with all the talent they had, why they didn't have a better team. Perhaps they were too hung up on a system. That's a common mistake for many young coaches.

Sometimes a coach is influenced too much by another coach. He might think, "Indiana won the championship with this formation," or "St. Louis did it that way, so if we can learn how to play that system . . . " yet he might not even have players who can play that style.

I've seen coaches insist on playing counterattack, fast-break soccer, for example, when they didn't have the speed up front to beat the opponent's defense. That approach is suicidal without superior speed. I've also seen coaches who insist on slowing the tempo by trying to build an attack through short passing combination play, but they don't have players with the ball-handling ability or the intelligence to create. They might be better off playing with fewer touches and trying to penetrate more quickly — not just kick and run, but use fewer passes to advance the ball.

The system must suit the players. The talent on hand and the opponent's tendencies should determine the approach a coach uses for the next game. If the opponent is weak defensively on the left side, a team can concentrate its attack on the right. If an opponent gives a team room at midfield, it should be able to play to the players' feet at midfield and do more combining. If the opponent plays a pressurizing zone defense, a team needs to be able to change the point of attack quickly by playing with fewer touches. Teams must be flexible enough to make adjustments according to the strategy of the opponent.

However, this does not necessarily apply to youth teams. Coaches tend to want to over-coach younger players and make it too complicated. The game itself is a great teacher. It's fun by its nature, and coaches of young players should not get too caught up in systems and formations. Coaches should place them in an area of the field and give them responsibilities, but at the same time not stifle their creativity.

Young players should be allowed to show creativity and express themselves within the game. I hate to hear a coach yelling, "Get back there, what are you doing dribbling like that?!" That's part of the joy of playing. The beehive approach kids take, running after the ball in clusters, is only natural because they want to be in the action. To tell a kid to stand back and play only when the ball is in his or her part of the field takes the fun out of the game and doesn't teach him or her much.

Youth coaches still can teach basic principles of play both offensively and defensively, but they should regognize stages of development. The beginning players shouldn't be burdened too much with strategies and roles and formations. They should simply be allowed to play.

● ● ●

Coaches should not overlook the basic nature of their players in determining how and where they best fit into the team. Different roles favor different personalities. A primary attacker generally has a different personality than a strong defender, for example, and to place a player in a role poorly suited for him can cause problems.

Not every position has a personality profile, but on advanced teams it is important to find at least one player who has a nose for the goal — someone who has a great hunger to score. I've had players up front who were excellent ballhandlers, who could beat people and unbalance defenses and create good scoring opportunities, but then would find a way *not* to score. In the final analysis, nothing happened.

However, a less skilled player who doesn't have the same flair to beat the defense might be able to make something happen on the occasions when he gets into scoring position because of his confidence and the sheer force of his will. Coaches should look for that personality in at least one player. If they can find more than one player with a scorer's mentality, it's a bonus.

Teams also need players on the flank who have the speed to burn a defense and the ability and willingness to serve balls to teammates. We've had players who didn't have great speed but had great one-on-one moves, and they took more satisfaction out of an assist than a shot. Coaches should try to find that kind of combination, one in which they have primary feeders and primary goal scorers working together.

Coaches should continually be searching for a blend of players who can do different things. If they have too many in the same area who like to do the same things and have the same personalities, the combination isn't likely to work very well. Coaches might have two gifted scorers they want playing in the same area of the field, but the result is like a magnet: the like poles repel each other rather than attract. Both players might be extremely talented, but that doesn't necessarily mean they can play well together.

A coach, for example, might think he wants his best ballhandlers to play together at midfield; however, it might be better to move one of them to an attacking position and bring in a player who complements the other ballhandler. The player brought in might not be as skilled, but perhaps he'll be the ball winner who helps set things up for the scorer. Establishing the right blend, the right chemistry, is crucial.

In the back, coaches should look for players who are stable, dependable and competitive — players who want to establish authority and dominate the opposing attackers. Hopefully, at least one of them is also able to bring the ball out of the back and distribute it to initiate the attack. This can be a sweeper or another back player.

However, some players don't have the personality traits necessary to excel defensively. They're creative free spirits who want to be closer to the opponent's goal, where improvisation is a virtue.

Teams also need players willing to do the dirty work, such as running down loose balls, winning the 50/50 balls and stopping opponents. These are the elements coaches must sort out. An individual's personality has a great deal to do with what role he should play for the team.

My 1991 team exemplified the importance of developing proper chemistry. After struggling early in the season to get our combinations working, we moved a player up front who had never played a forward position; he had always been a midfielder or a defender. He was less gifted than the player he replaced, but his presence up front made the team more effective. He brought a fight and a spirit to the attack that lifted the other players. He didn't have the same flair with the ball as the other players, but his work ethic was infectious.

Because of our interchangeable approach, we generally don't recruit by position, except in the case of goaltenders. It often takes quite awhile to determine the position for which a player is best suited. Many of our excellent defenders were forwards in high school, for example. We try to find the best total soccer players, bring them in and teach them our system and our principles of play, and see what fits their personalities.

The coach's association with his players also comes into play here. If he has established a comfortable rapport with them, he can more accurately detect their personality traits and determine where they can contribute most on the field.

I also believe each team has an overall personality, and that should be considered in choosing its particular style. Of my three NCAA championship teams, the 1988 team had a different personality than the first two. It was more of a blue collar team. The players worked hard for each other, and didn't necessarily win by having more skill than their opponents. We had some great individual talent on that team, but not as much as the other two championship teams.

My championship teams in 1982 and '83, and the one that was runner-up in '84, relied more on raw talent. It seemed as though the best thing that could happen to them was for their opponent to score a goal early in the game; it was almost like they needed a wake-up call. They had a tremendous amount of confidence in each other and it showed on the field. They intimidated their opponents and wore them down mentally. The '88 team, on the other hand, simply outworked its opponents and wore them down physically. They kept coming and kept coming and never gave up. They seemed stronger toward the end of the games, and won a lot of games in the closing minutes.

•  •  •

The NCAA recently passed a rule limiting practice for Division I programs to 20 hours per week during the season. Some coaches aren't pleased with the cutbacks, but the NCAA might have done them a favor.

Longer is not necessarily better when it comes to practice. When I was starting out, I thought if I wasn't out there at least two hours or more I wasn't a good coach. But I've come to realize over the years that a practice does not need to last longer than 90 minutes if it is well-organized.

Our practices now are more streamlined, and they are better as a result. The players stay fresher throughout the season. They also are more enthusiastic about what they're doing when they know the practice won't drag on forever. Coaches at all levels should realize they can get their work done

in a relatively short amount of time if they are properly organized. Keep the practices short and sweet whenever possible.

Coaches also should be flexible with their practice schedules. The best-laid plans on paper don't always work out well on the field. Sometimes coaches think they're being unorganized if they deviate from their schedule, but I consider that to be flexible and creative. A coach has to be able to adjust to his team's needs. Why emphasize ball control one day because the schedule he drew up several weeks ago says to, when recent games have made it clear the team needs to work on finishing or defense? A common sense approach works best.

As a young coach, I would outline a practice that included everything I wanted to cover. Then, even if the players struggled with something after we got on the field, I would stubbornly stick with the schedule. Sometimes a coach just has to scrap his plan and go on. I still map out our practice sessions, but I make it a point to remain flexible. It's not cast in stone by any means.

A coach must have a feel for the team. At times the players become psychologically stale; a coach must recognize this and make changes accordingly. Coaches cannot expect players to perform the same drills over and over again without losing interest after awhile. They must show variety and creativity in coming up with new activities and challenges so that practice is not too boring. At the same time, however, they cannot let a session become a circus. The trick is to find a balance between being well-organized and creative.

We try to take full advantage of the time before the official start of practice. Say, for example, most of the players arrive on the field, dressed and taped, at 3 o'clock, with the first formal activity not scheduled until 3:30. Each player, after proper warmup, should have an assigned activity to concentrate on during that pre-practice period to help improve his weaknesses. Too often players want to work only on their strengths when they are on their own. In excess, this amounts to little more than showing off. Coaches should make sure they are working to improve their weaknesses as well.

Many of the pre-practice activities can be done in small groups. For example, a player who is exceptionally strong at heading can work with teammates who are weak in that area. This is a free period, but should be organized sufficiently so that the players know what they must work on, and can do so without a coach directing them.

At 3:30, we would begin the formal practice by stretching as a group. Stretching is vital to the prevention of injuries and developing flexibility, therefore we treat this time seriously and use a full regimen of exercises.

This warmup phase can be completed with an activity that demands moderate movement. It should be an enjoyable activity that helps bring the warmup to a climax and encompasses various elements of the game. Playing five-on-two with a one- or two-touch restriction is a good activity for this purpose.

The next phase, which lasts 15-20 minutes, is devoted to the technical emphasis of the day, which would be a specific skill. We set up two or three stations, with a coach or player in charge at each one. If the emphasis for the day is heading, one station might concentrate on defensive heading, clearing the ball out high and wide. Another station could include services to the near or far post for heading on the goal. Each player, depending on his position or role for the team, should spend the appropriate amount of time at each station.

The next phase of training can be devoted to small group work and principles of play. This generally involves breaking the game down to its essential element — one-on-one offensive and defensive principles — so a great deal of time should be spent on activities that match one player against another. Use full-sized goals manned with keepers whenever possible, and try to incorporate a finish on goal with as many activities as possible.

We like to build up to two-on-three, three-on-two, three-on-four and four-on-three activities during this phase, and then continue building to larger groups — perhaps even a full-sided scrimmage. The game itself is a great teacher. It also is beneficial to impose conditions on individual players, or the entire team during the scrimmages to enhance learning, such as one- or two-touch restrictions.

If John is holding on to the ball too long during games, for example, we would impose the restriction that he must play one- or two-touch during the scrimmage. If Charlie is playing hot potato with the ball, we would require that he beat a man before he delivers a pass or shot. Defenders can be required to build up out of the back or bypass midfield.

Small-sided games, such as six-on-six, can be used in a confined area to concentrate on possession and combination play. Again, conditions can be set, such as allowing shots on goal only after a certain number of consecutive passes or touches.

Shadow play, in which the offense is set up to play against a limited number of defenders, can also be effective. The numbers can be increased progressively. The offense, for example, can work five-on-six or six-on-five, with the back four and one or two midfielders working against the attacking six. This can be done in a half-field situation with a particular mode of attack, such as having the front players work to create space for a midfielder coming through. Or, the midfielders can carry the ball into attack with the defense adjusting accordingly.

The point here is that scrimmages — short-sided or full-sided — aren't just games, they are opportunities to develop a tactical plan.

Restarts — free kicks, corner kicks and throw-ins — can be worked on during the pre-practice phase, and then later be incorporated into the more functional group activities.

Although I prefer to incorporate conditioning into the various phases of our practices, some coaches set aside specific time for it. If so, I believe it should be reserved for the final part of practice, therefore the players are fresh mentally and physically while practicing techniques and principles at the early stages of the practice session. Speed work can be scattered throughout the practice, but heavy fitness training should be done at the end of the session.

Coaches differ in regard to how much time players should spend scrimmaging. I'm an advocate of scrimmaging. The players are out there because they love to play the game. They've been playing it most of their lives and they enjoy it. Sometimes coaches get carried away with their practice plans. They forget why the players are there and what their primary objective is, which is to have fun and play the game.

That's one thing I've learned, and try to keep in mind at all times. Practice can't become a circus; it can't just be "fun day" everyday. But I work hard at trying to make sure the players enjoy it. And the one activity they enjoy the most is playing the game. Ask players what they want to do and they'll say, "Let's scrimmage!" They want to play, so we let them play. But we teach within the scrimmages.

Some coaches believe it's a waste of time to conduct full scrimmages. They don't believe they get any teaching accomplished, that they lose control. I disagree. I believe the game is the best teacher. Players can best rehearse tactics, establish tempo of play and work on combination play through scrimmages. It's one thing to look good in two-on-two situations or small group practice, but that doesn't always carry over to games.

Generally, our most recent game indicates what we need to work on during practice. We'll use video tapes to learn more about our strengths and weaknesses, and to check our statistics. If we are turning the ball over too much, we'll work on improving ball control. We'll set up activities that are relevant to our needs at the time.

●  ●  ●

The psychological aspects of coaching any sport are a real challenge. A coach wants to discover the key to each individual. How can he open that kid up? How does he get to him? With some kids it's a pat on the back, with others it's a stern hand. A coach needs to gain his athletes' trust so they'll work hard for him.

To do that, a coach must react to the players individually. He can't treat everyone the same. He must have the same rules and policies for everyone, but he has to adjust to individual personalities. Finding the best means of motivating each individual is a real key to building a successful team. A coach can have the greatest talent in the world, but if he can't reach the players — if he can't keep them motivated — he won't be successful.

One important method of motivation is to keep the practices competitive. We try to set things up so that our practices are more difficult than our games, and we make it clear to the players that positions can be won and lost in practice. If players start thinking they have their spot secure and don't have to work hard in training, then the coach has problems.

I like for a player to know that if he lets down there's somebody right there on his heels ready to take over. When that situation is established, a coach finds he doesn't have many players missing training; the injuries don't seem to occur as frequently, especially the psychological ones. Also, the overall effort put forth in practice is stronger. If the coach can keep the competition keen within his own team, it strengthens the team in many ways, both physically and psychologically.

The coach must also work to create an environment that helps the athletes develop confidence. He can do this in the way he conducts the practice sessions, and how he structures the team. However, as in the case of leadership, each team needs one or two team members who raise the confidence level of everyone. The coach can orchestrate it to a degree, but it has to come from within. It's like a symphony in some respects. The coach can provide direction, but the players have to want to perform.

Before a game, I'll talk about what we need to do, and perhaps about the importance of a game. I've also brought in guests, such as Coach Knight, to talk to my players — someone to add variety and give them something new to think about.

I used to give rah-rah talks in my early coaching years, but I've come to realize that the higher-level players have their own way of getting ready for the game. A couple of them might sit quietly in the corner, while others might be pumping each other up. A coach should allow for individual differences. Of course there might be some who need a spark, and a coach has to be able to provide that for them.

Overall, though, I'm not a cheerleader. I don't have my players running through walls to get to the field. That just doesn't fit me. They'd laugh at me if I tried it. But I do get intense. I love to compete, and that rubs off on the players. One of my teams in the early years gave me a plaque that read, "To Coach Yeagley, who has a burning desire to achieve." I believe that most teams reflect the personality of their head coach; the coach sets the mood. Yet all coaches must recognize the need to operate within their personality. If they don't, they'll wind up looking foolish.

The coach should also establish a sportsmanlike atmosphere. This should go without saying, but there are teams at every level, from youth leagues to professionals, that lack basic sportsmanship. Everyone wants to win, of course, but they should want to do it within the rules and do it with class. This is particularly important in youth leagues. It's disheartening to see coaches at that level screaming at their players, the opponent or at the officials. At that level more than any other, the coaches should focus on instilling sportsmanship.

The attitude toward the opponent, the officials and the game has to remain a positive one. It's ridiculous to try to find ways of getting around the rules or to try to physically eliminate an opponent. Coaches and players all have moments when they are reminded of soccer's overall place in the world. They should keep this in mind at all times.

• • •

If a coach is fortunate enough to enjoy continued success, he is faced with a new problem: complacency. As far as problems go, this is a good one to have, because it means he's accomplished something. But he must find ways to deal with it, both from within himself and his players.

A team is bound to have valleys of fatigue during a season, whether it is winning or not. Players get psychologically stale, and the coach must look out for that. Over the years the signs become apparent. The players might be arguing among themselves and appear to be losing their enthusiasm. They get grouchy. There are all kinds of tell-tale signs.

A coach can deal with this in one of two ways. He can crack the whip, or he can do something to break the monotony and give the players a new outlook. My approach in the early years was to bear down on the players even harder. We'd train longer and work harder when I thought the players were losing some of their intensity. Now I often go the other way. I might

give them a day off, or I'll have them do something like play soccer volleyball; something not directly related to the game, but something different and fun. If it's a wet day, we might practice dive headers and slide tackles in the mud. Or we might make the practices shorter.

At times such as these, a coach needs to throw away the plan for the moment and realize he's got a more important problem: getting his team back on track. A lot of times changing the environment and changing the activities does the trick. This comes from experience. It's a feel a coach acquires, and he has to know when to trust his judgement.

I've even done this before some very important games. The assistants might say, "We've got a huge game coming up and you want to cut practice to 45 minutes? We need to be working harder." But at a late point in the season the players can't be taught much of anything new. They aren't likely to improve a great deal with an extra hour of work at that point. They need to be refreshed mentally. It's a gamble, but with experience a coach develops a feel for his team's moods.

We start practice in mid-August and go two times a day. I can almost guarantee that by mid-September we'll have a stale period, and then two-thirds of the way through the season we'll have another one, and then at tournament time we'll have another one. People might think when a team is preparing for the tournament it should be getting psyched up, but it might be better to take some time off to get refreshed.

• • •

Soccer is a player's game. The coaching must be done during the week; after that the games are in the players' hands. In international competition coaches aren't even allowed to actively coach on the sidelines. We're allowed to do more in college, but many times the yelling, the *attempted* coaching, does more harm than good because the players have trouble focusing on the game.

A coach can substitute and make minor adjustments at halftime, but for the most part he turns the game over to his players and hopes they're prepared for all the situations they might encounter during a game.

This brings up the subject of "big games," which all coaches face. For a youth league coach, a big game might be one against the team that leads the division, or against the crosstown rival. Whatever a team's level, it will play some games that are more important than others, for various reasons.

The approach for games such as these should not change drastically. We lost in the final game of the NCAA tournament in 1976, '78 and '80 before we won our first championship in 1982. I don't think we did anything much differently when we won the titles as opposed to when we finished second. If anything, we probably focused more on what we did well rather than on the opponent. Teams must prepare for opponents and know their tendencies, but after losing in the championship game three times we realized we had to be primarily concerned with our own play.

Of course, after losing a championship game three times a coach becomes concerned about "choking." That's not a term I like, because it's not fair to the defeated team. The loser of a big game does not necessarily "choke." However, coaches and athletes can't help but doubt themselves a bit after they've lost some big games. Winning that first championship got a big monkey off our back, but coaches must realize some things are out of their control. All they can do is prepare their team as well as possible and let the chips fall.

I learned that lesson in 1979, when my team reached the final eight of the NCAA tournament before losing at Penn State. Our team had 18 shutouts during the season. No NCAA team has ever had more than that. We just dominated our opponents and played beautiful soccer all season, but we ran out of luck at Penn State.

It was one of the most disheartening losses I've had as a coach. We had snow flurries that day, and there was an icy crust on the field. We just couldn't score. It was a game that everyone expected Indiana to win, but we didn't.

It was a tribute to our team, at least, that Penn State carried its goalkeeper off the field. Anytime the opposing team's goalkeeper is the hero of the match, a team knows it did some things right. Their goalkeeper had a magical night, and several of our shots deflected off the posts.

If people had watched that game and not seen the goals, and had then been asked to pick the winner, there's no doubt most of them would have chosen Indiana as the winner. But that's the nature of soccer. Penn State was a great team, too, but I think a lot of people agree that perhaps the nation's top team didn't win the championship that year. That happens in all sports, though, and it usually evens out over the long run.

For us, the key to success in the championship games was making it a point to be the aggressor. At Indiana we take great pride in having opponents say they weren't able to *play their game*, that they had a bad day.

That's a great compliment to our team because we stress defense so much. We try to make a team play the way we want them to play, rather than falling back and letting them do what they want to do and trying to stop them at that.

In our third national championship game, against San Francisco in 1980, we concentrated on taking their game away from them. We wanted to determine how the game was going to be played and get the psychological edge on them. We lost that game in overtime, but we were more competitive, and we carried that lesson into our subsequent championship games.

Our loss in the 1980 championship game brought about another challenge: overcoming disappointment. We had a two-goal lead and never expected to lose, but we made a couple of mistakes that allowed them to tie the game. It was our mistakes that cost us, not their big plays. We had nobody to blame for the loss but ourselves. We simply got careless.

First, we knocked in a goal ourselves to give San Francisco their first goal. It started with an errant back pass. One of our players knocked the ball back to our goalkeeper and didn't see they had a player nearby. That began a domino effect. Our other defender came in to try to save the ball and he collided with the goalkeeper and the ball was knocked loose. It could be called a fluke, but we made the fluke occur. We had been completely in control of the game up to that point.

Then, when our heads were still down from giving up a silly goal, two of our players sandwiched one of their players in the penalty area, resulting in a foul and setting up a penalty kick for a goal. There was a direct relationship between the two events. Rather than saying "OK, we made a mistake, let's get our heads up, we're still ahead," we fouled them and suddenly it's 2-2 at halftime.

At halftime I couldn't get their chins up off the floor. It was an incredibly frustrating situation. We thought we had the game won and that we were a much better team, and suddenly we were in trouble. I tried to make the players realize we were still tied, that it was anybody's game. But San Francisco came back out and scored shortly after the start of the second half. We tied the game, 3-3, but later lost in overtime. It was a tough way to lose.

A lot of lessons were learned in that game. First, obviously, a team must be extremely careful about passing the ball back to the goalkeeper. A lot of things can go wrong, as we proved. Beyond that, however, we didn't react

properly to our mistake. We still had a 2-1 lead and were in control of the game after that mistake, but we lost our composure and that led to their second goal. We let it bother us too much, and as a result we didn't come out the second half ready to play.

Experience is another important factor in big games. Aside from the obvious fact that older players usually are more talented, they are also more likely to be poised in pressure situations. This was proven in 1991, when we advanced to the Final Four and played Santa Clara. We had five or six first-year players in the lineup, and they had seven senior starters.

For the first 15 or 20 minutes we played at least even with them. Then they scored on a throw-in in our defensive third of the field. Our players' heads dropped; they weren't mature enough or experienced enough to bounce back from it. Santa Clara's seniors realized that was an opportunity to put us away, and they took control of the game. After that goal we had some opportunities, but for the most part that goal was the turning point. Our team did a great job and overachieved for the most part that season, but the youth and inexperience showed. I think they learned from it.

A coach can't do a lot about situations like these during games. He can't control experience, and he can't call timeouts, so he just has to hope there's enough leadership on the field to meet the challenges. But a coach can't manufacture leadership if it isn't there. All he can do is identify it and allow it to come to the forefront when it is ready to surface.

The importance of leadership was exemplified by one of our players in the early 1980s, John Stollmeyer. It is no coincidence that in the four years he played for us we played in three national championship games, and won two of them. He was more than a great player, he was an inspirational leader. The players feared letting him down as much as they did the coaches.

That kind of leadership is rare, but if a coach is fortunate to have a player with those qualities, he shouldn't be afraid to let him lead. Insecure coaches might worry about giving up part of their authority to a player. That's a mistake. A team needs more leadership than a coach can provide by himself, and there are times — particularly during games — when a leader on the field can do more for the team than a coach can.

• • •

At higher levels of collegiate soccer, substitutions are quite limited. Many times coaches don't make any, and most teams have just two or three players that are used frequently off the bench in close games. Mass substitution is not as prevalent as it is used to be.

In the early years of our program, because our talent didn't match up well with many of our opponents, we had to have our players do a lot more running, so we substituted more. Now that we match up favorably in personnel, we don't substitute much at all.

This means players have to earn their positions in practice. It also means the coach does most of his work in practice, and then the players take over in the games. The coach can still make changes during a game if someone is not playing well. Sometimes making a substitution can change the momentum.

A coach also might have two players very similar in ability who he wants to share playing time. Also, some players — particularly younger players — might not have the fitness level to play 90 minutes. Teams occasionally have situations where they play two or three games a week, or have a weekend tournament in which they play more than one game a day. Some situations demand that more substitutions be made.

Still, at higher levels, teams need to develop a flow, a tempo. This is more difficult to achieve if continuous substitutions are being made. It depends on the level of play, of course. Youth leagues, high schools and some colleges emphasize participation, so coaches at those levels might want to substitute more often. Participation is important, but a better way to guarantee that is to have more teams with fewer players, rather than having a lot of players playing only segments of each game.

We'll have some players on our 25-man roster who go through a season and play very little. That's a difficult situation for them. They have to practice hard like the rest of the team, but they don't get to taste much of the glory. This is an obvious reason not to have a large squad size. It's also a valid justification for having junior varsity games to help keep everyone involved and happy. The players who aren't playing shouldn't be put in a situation where they might damage the entire team's morale. The coach should explain his philosophy to the reserve players and make clear to them their role on the team.

However, we might not start the same 11 players every game. If someone has a poor game, or is not putting forth the effort in practice, we'll make a change. The bench can be a great motivator for talented players who aren't playing up to their potential. I worry when we have a situation, either because of lack of depth or numerous injuries, where a player feels he can put forth less than his best effort and still remain in the game, or play in the next one.

• • •

One of the great things about coaching is that every season presents a new challenge. It's never the same. It's not a typical 8-5 job. A coach deals with different problems, and must come up with different approaches to motivation and to training. He needs to find ways to keep training activities interesting, challenging and enjoyable. It's difficult for veteran coaches to do that over a long period of time.

It's important for coaches to enjoy what they're doing. That might sound simplistic, but a lot of coaches get burned out and go through the motions, just as players do. If they genuinely love their jobs, however, they should have no problem keeping their emotions high. Coaches who find they have lost their drive and desire should consider moving on to something else.

Every coach has a level where he fits in best. Some work best with beginning players, others with professionals, others somewhere in between. In some part it depends on their personality. I happen to work best with college players.

Every coach should find the level where he is most comfortable and try to work there. It doesn't have to be at the major college or professional level. A coach can have a rewarding career whether he is coaching young kids or high school players. I know I'm glad Barney Hoffman stayed at the high school level. A coach can influence lives at any level, so he shouldn't get hung up on "getting to the top" of the profession. The top is where he is happiest. And the happier he is, the better he will perform as a coach.

I almost left to take a professional coaching job once. It would have paid much more than I was making as a college coach at the time and it seemed like a great opportunity, but it would have been a big mistake for me. At Indiana I'm working with an age group that I enjoy working with and I have a chance to affect their lives and witness the rewards of it. I hear now from guys who played 10 or 15 years ago. They talk about their jobs and their

family and sometimes they thank me and tell me how much their participation in the soccer program meant to them, both on the field and off the field.

That, after 30 years of coaching, is as important as what is happening now on the field. I'm as competitive as ever, but the rewards now also come from the products of the program. It's like having children grow up and become successful. That's a great satisfaction for a coach, and shouldn't be taken for granted.

# Offense

**M**y philosophy toward soccer is very simple. When the opponent has the ball, we want everyone putting 100 percent into defense, both mentally and physically. When we have possession, we want everyone putting 100 percent of their concentration into offense.

As stated in the previous chapter, we want everyone sharing in the attack, with as much interchange as possible. The difficult thing is getting and developing players with the overall skills to play such a system, and then teaching them how to execute it. Obviously, all 10 field players can't be going forward in attack at the same time. Some have to stay back to give the team proper balance and shape. The challenge is to teach them when to go forward and when to stay back. But if a team can generate offense from its back players as well as its front players, it is that much more difficult to defend.

Regardless of a team's offensive style, it should be able to vary the tempo of play. It should be able to build the attack slowly, penetrate quickly and take advantage of what opponents allow. Opponents will defend in different ways, sometimes even during the course of a single game. Coaches must be able to recognize this and take advantage of what's being given. If the opponent allows outside play, for example, or if it allows the backs a great deal of room, the attacking team must be able to react accordingly.

Teams can always learn of an opponent's tendencies from advance scouting, but they must be able to react to changes that occur during games. Players must be trained to do so during practice. Intelligence and recognition are crucial assets for a soccer player.

• • •

Regardless of a team's offensive style, certain principles hold true for most everyone. Two or more team members can create space for themselves through combination play and intelligent movement with and without the ball.

## Overlap runs

Overlap runs are made from positions behind the ball. They usually are made from wide positions, near the touch lines, but also can be made in more central locations. The player in possession of the ball must advance slowly, so that the overlapping player can advance around the ballhandler and move toward the live space they are trying to attack.

Communication is important between the two players. The overlapping player must tell the player in possession of the ball to hold the ball while he advances into position. The overlapping player's run should be to the outside of the ballhandler in order to create the best angle for receiving the pass and to give the overlapping player better field vision as he receives the ball.

The player in possession must be careful not to telegraph the pass to the overlapping player by revealing his intention. He also must be careful not to deliver the pass too early or too late. The best time to serve the ball into the attacking space is after the overlapping player comes into the ballhandler's peripheral vision. If the ball is served too late, the overlapping player might be offside; if it is served too soon, the pass might be intercepted.

## Takeover plays

Takeover plays are designed to draw two defenders close together, creating confusion and thus creating space for the attackers. Takeover plays can be completed in a side-to-side (across the field) fashion or end-to-end (down the field).

The player in possession of the ball and his teammate move toward each other and cross paths. As they cross, the player not in possession either takes the ball from his teammate or acts as a decoy as his teammate continues to carry the ball into the attack.

The two crossing players must communicate with each other so that they know which of them will have possession of the ball at the moment of the potential takeover. I prefer that the player with the best field of vision determine who keeps possession. This generally is the player not dribbling. If this player determines it is best for him to take possession, he says, "Leave!" as he nears his teammate. If he decides it is best for him not to

take possession, he remains silent. Unsuccessful takeover plays usually are the result of confusion between the two players. The player with the ball should leave it for his teammate to pick up rather than try to touch it to him.

It also is important for both players to accelerate at the point of the takeover, regardless of which one has possession. The player with possession as the two players approach must be careful to shield the ball by dribbling with the foot furthest from his opponent.

## Penetration

The objective of all attacking teams, unless they are killing the clock, is to move the ball toward the opponent's goal. This is called penetration. To achieve penetration, teams must be able to make forward, positive passes to teammates making hard, accelerated runs into the attacking space.

Early penetration is at the heart of successful counterattacking. The more time the defense is allowed to retreat and get players goalside of the ball, the more difficult it is to make successful penetrating passes. Late penetration often results in failure because the defense has been given time to set up.

Well-timed and early penetrating passes will bypass most defensive players and hopefully result in one-on-one opportunities heading toward goal. It is not always possible to play the ball forward immediately, however, so it is sometimes necessary to play the ball back first to create a better penetrating pass.

The most effective penetrating passes are usually those from a wide position to the center of the field, rather than from the center toward the flank.

## Width in attack

A primary objective for any attacking team is to create space. Too often, however, teams become congested in one area of the field and do not take advantage of the width. Spreading out from side to side is one of the best ways to create space and create a more difficult situation for defenders to cover and provide support.

Achieving width enables teams to attack from the flanks toward the center of the field. Players bunching in the center of the field is one of the biggest obstacles coaches face.

## Wall pass

The wall pass, also known as the one-two, is a fundamental aspect in attacking play. It is a simple give-and-go maneuver in which a player passes the ball to a teammate, then sprints into an open space to receive a quick return pass.

The maneuver is quite effective, but requires proper timing between the two players. They also must be able to execute the play in close quarters.

The player making the initial pass should try to disguise it. An outside-of-the-foot pass is often the most effective method of doing so. He should make the pass to the wall player's closest foot. He then should immediately accelerate to receive the return pass. The first two steps of the movement, including the foot making the initial pass, are the most important. The second pass is made to space for the first player to run on to.

The wall player also should roll off the defender immediately after passing to the cutting player to try to find space for himself. Too many times the wall player stands and watches, failing to take advantage of an opportunity to receive another return pass.

The passes must be crisp and executed with proper pace. They should be made on the first touch to be effective, and usually are most effectively executed on the ground.

## One-touch passing

As players advance to higher levels, they must be able to play accurate one-touch soccer as they close on their opponent's goal. Many golden scoring opportunities are missed because the receiving player must make an extra touch to control the ball. Players must be able to see the field and make an early decision so that they know what they will do with the ball before they receive it.

One-touch (or first-time) play encourages players to constantly survey the field and make decisions before they receive the ball, as well as to keep moving so that they will be in position to receive a pass.

It is important to change the point of attack through a series of one-touch interpassing. The defense cannot react nearly as quickly to a ball passed in one-touch fashion as they can to a player who is dribbling the ball. One-touch passing also requires players to move into proper supporting positions very quickly to help the player receiving the ball. It also encourages and requires players to move into new supporting positions as soon as they have played the ball.

One-touch play is not popular among most players because it is both physically and mentally demanding. Ample practice time should be devoted to improving one-touch skills.

## Mobility and blind-side runs

To successfully attack concentrated defenses, players must be mobile and unpredictable. Attacking players make a defender's job relatively easy if they remain stationary in front of the defender. Being creative individually by finding ways to get through the defense with unexpected moves is an important element of improvisation. The great attackers find ways to beat a defense when no openings appear available. It's a spontaneous move that isn't planned and perhaps not even practiced, but draws upon the player's skill and instinct.

Blind-side runs are a common method of executing unpredictable maneuvers. Movement made behind the defense away from the ball places defenders under intense pressure, and can open up space for the attackers.

Blind-side runs are generally instinctive moves made according to what the defense allows. If defenders focus too much on play around the ball — get caught ball-watching — and lose track of other attackers, they leave themselves vulnerable to blind-side runs. Attackers should be looking for every opportunity to slip behind their marker and find open space to receive a pass.

An effective blind-side run in the attacking third requires the runner to have good vision and timing, as well as the ability to finish. Blind-side runs are effective maneuvers in any area of the field, however. They are most commonly made from the flank toward the center of the field, but can be made diagonally from the center toward the flank.

Runners must remember that their efforts often will not bring a pass. The player in possession of the ball might not see the runner in time to make a pass, if he sees him at all, or the ballhandler might choose to make another play. Still, players must be willing to make runs whenever they are appropriate. Even if they do not receive a pass, they can contribute to the attack by stretching the defense and creating an opening for a teammate. Even the mere threat of a blind-side run can assist the attack because it keeps the defense spread wider, thus increasing the chances of finding open attacking space.

● ● ●

I prefer that my teams play a short passing, ball control game, keeping the ball on the ground but mixing in direct play utilizing quick penetrating ability. That's not unusual, but to try to impose such a style on players who are not prepared for it can be very frustrating. Coaches can try to encourage and develop a certain style of play, but they must first determine what the players are capable of doing and try to build from there.

In my early years as a coach, when we did not have great talent, we were a defensive-oriented, counterattacking team. We generated much of our attack by inviting the opponent to attack us, forcing them into mistakes and countering quickly. We didn't have the talent to match up all over the field with our opponents then, but we did have good speed up front.

We used that tactic when Angelo DiBernardo, a freshman, scored five goals against St. Louis in 1976. Nobody had ever scored five goals against St. Louis before. The game was played on artificial turf in our football stadium, so that catered to his speed.

Sixty to 70 percent of that game was played in our defensive half, with St. Louis in control of the ball, and yet we scored five counterattack goals. Angelo stayed up top, while our defense didn't allow them high percentage scoring chances. As soon as we won the ball we looked for Angelo and got the ball to him in the open field. We kept him at midfield, as his job was to be in the best position on the receiving end of a penetrating pass as soon as we won possession. As a result, we were able to get him one-on-one against a defender in a foot race to goal.

Today we play a different style because we have better overall talent, but DiBernardo was truly gifted and we wanted to take advantage of his ability. We wanted to give the opponent a false sense of security by inviting them into our half of the field and then give Angelo the entire half of the field to attack against one or two defenders.

In those days we were trying to generate a lot of our offense off the other team's mistakes. This is a suitable strategy for teams that are outmanned by their opponent. Now, because we have better talent and can match up with our opponents, we try to dictate how we want to play on offense and change the tempo depending on what the opponents give us.

That's part of the chess game, seeing what is available that day and taking advantage of it, while trying to take away the opponent's favored style of play. Our midfielders and backs now contribute up to 50 percent of our scoring, while in our early days 90 percent of our scoring came from our front players.

Coaches must assess their players' skills and potential, and then determine how they should generate the attack. Trying to mount a counterattack as the primary offensive tactic is foolish if a team does not have extremely quick players up front. The speed of the front players determines to a large extent if a team will be successful using the counterattack tactic.

Our current approach to offense, which incorporates everyone into the offense, paid off in 1982, when Gregg Thompson, a defender, scored both of our goals in a 2-1, eight-overtime win over Duke in the national championship game. Gregg was one of our best defenders and he was marking one of Duke's top scorers, but when we had the ball he was expected to join the attack at the appropriate time.

He scored a great goal off of a throw-in from about 20 yards out. Then he scored on a free kick to win the game in the eighth overtime. Gregg practiced that free kick everyday. It didn't happen by chance.

He was a great role model and inspiration for our other players. Gregg came to practice earlier, stayed later and worked harder than the others so that when his chance did come he'd be ready for it. It did come, and he was ready. He went on to become the NASL Rookie of the Year and played for the United States in the 1984 Olympics.

As a coach, it's a tremendous thrill seeing guys like that succeed, because they deserve every bit of the success they get. Gregg Thompson served as an excellent role model to everyone because of his strong work ethic. He didn't have great size, but he worked hard at weight training and became very strong. And his work ethic toward skill development — in this case the free kick — paid off handsomely.

We had a similar situation occur in our 1983 championship win over Columbia, when Pat McGauley scored the only goal of the game in the second overtime. Pat had gone through a scoring drought at the end of the season. He was one of our key forwards, but he was struggling. A lot of players would have gotten down on themselves and let it affect their play, but he hung in there. He worked through the drought and put forth the extra effort to score the game-winner.

This a lesson for all players regarding persistence. No matter how talented a player is, he is bound to have slumps. However, he can't let it affect his intensity or confidence. And coaches must have patience with players who are struggling, as long as they have proven their talent in the past. We had been telling Pat he was going to get a goal when it really counted, and he did. He put forth a great deal of effort to reach a cross that wasn't certain of even getting through to him.

• • •

A team's playing style might need to change during a game, depending on the situations that arise. A team that is leading with 10 or 15 minutes to go, for example, should not take unnecessary risks. Perhaps it commits fewer players to its attack to help avoid exposing itself and allowing a possible scoring opportunity for the other team. Teams should know how to kill the clock.

At the same time, teams must be careful when they have the lead to continue playing to win, rather than playing not to lose. The team with the lead can't just sit back. It must continue to play aggressively and positively, but avoid putting itself at risk. The shift in playing style when a team has the lead should be minor, not drastic.

Teams that are behind need to be able to make adjustments as well. Something we do is go "even numbers" by playing without our sweeper. We did that in 1984 in the championship game when we were trailing 1-0 with about 15 minutes remaining. We had prepared for this type of situation in practice. By pulling a sweeper out and putting another player in, we were able to go head-to-head with the opponent all over the field. We were able to force some turnovers, then we drew a foul, got a free kick and tied the score 1-1.

We also go even numbers if we aren't generating offense during a game and we need to create a change in momentum. It is important to remember, however, that a team makes itself more vulnerable to conceding a goal by removing the sweeper.

If a team is trailing, but generating good scoring opportunities, there is no need to go even numbers until about 15 minutes remain in the game. If a team is not generating offense, however, it might be wise to go to it earlier.

Weather conditions and the field surface can also cause a change in playing style. Wind, rain, snow, hard ground, soft ground, the size of the field, the height of the grass, artificial turf — all these are conditions that can affect how a team approaches the game.

If a team is playing on a heavy field or a wet field, it might be advantageous to go to a more direct game, with more long passes and less dribbling and short passes. Some coaches whose teams are more effective when playing at a slow tempo have been known to keep the grass on their field a bit higher to help slow down play. Artificial turf, on the other hand, favors teams with superior running speed.

Teams playing on a windy day should try to keep the ball out of the air, or take advantage of the conditions by putting the ball up near the opponent's goal area if they have tall people who can dominate there.

Games on a narrow field might force teams to play a more direct style, with the ball in the air more. Teams that play on high school football fields don't have much width to work with, which makes it difficult to open up combination play through the midfield.

• • •

When a team gains possession of the ball, its players should initially read how the opponent is defending and take advantage of what is available. Everyone must concentrate on how they can take the situation and turn it to their advantage as quickly as possible. Where should they be moving without the ball? Where should they be moving to provide support?

If you are playing a team that gives you even numbers — for example, one that plays without a deep sweeper and does not have good cover in the back — you must recognize this and try to serve the ball to your front players, who can go one-on-one.

If your opponent uses zone principles, then your players should play the ball more to each other's feet and change the point of attack quickly. Zone defense allows that space of three or four yards when players are moving from one zonal area to the next. Against a zone, players must work hard to find blind side positions to open the space they need to receive the ball.

When playing against a team employing strict man-to-man defense, players should make unselfish runs to create space for other players who are not tightly marked. Players also must work hard at running their defenders into less dangerous space, space that they do not want to exploit, to open up space in front of the opponent's goal, and then find ways to serve the ball to teammates in that area.

A team cannot go into a game and simply say, "We're going to play our game." If a team is that much better than its opponent it might be able to do that, but at higher levels of play it is not a practical approach. When teams are roughly equal in talent, players must recognize what's being given to them.

A team should not try to force balls to its front players if it has two front players against four back players. On the other hand, it shouldn't try to build up slowly if it is given even numbers up front; in such a situation it must play the ball forward and penetrate early.

Ideally, a team will be versatile in its offensive approach and be able to do what the game dictates: build up, play direct, come from behind, or create space for front, midfield or back players.

If a team is unfamiliar with its opponent, the first 10 to 15 minutes of a match is a sparring process, a time to sort out what type of defense it is up against. Whichever team can establish the tempo of play generally will be successful.

If a team is struggling against an opponent's defense, individual creativity might help it overcome the situation. If the defense allows space for the backs to operate and then suddenly cuts it off, for example, it would be foolish to try to keep forcing the ball out of the back. Against Hartwick in the semifinal of the 1984 NCAA tournament, and then against Clemson in the final, our backs did not have the opportunity to build out of the back; both teams had devised defenses that kept them out of our attack. That meant, however, that we had players open in the midfield. We recognized that a little too late in the final game against Clemson, which we lost 2-1, but we made some adjustments at halftime and were able to generate some strong attacks.

Players must be willing to take risks in the offensive third of the field. They are likely to be up against even numbers or perhaps an extra defender there, so individual creativity is an important asset. Players must be willing to challenge defenders and risk losing possession in the offensive third of the field.

The principles of improvisation — doing the unexpected — come into play here. There is less space to work in, so a team's offensive options are limited. Top attackers can unbalance the defense by beating their defender, then draw the extra player (the sweeper) to give their team even numbers — which usually is all any team can hope for in attack.

Players must assume the responsibility of attempting to beat players one-on-one, and coaches must assume the responsibility of training their players against numbers that favor the defense. Practice time should be devoted to getting the ball behind the defense on the flanks and then serving balls to both the near and far post, on the ground and in the air.

The timing of runs is another important phase of attack, and should receive considerable attention in practice. Players without the ball must learn when to make their move. Players must learn in practice how to communicate during games, either by word or by signal to coordinate attacking runs.

Too often players are caught standing in front of the goal in the space their team wants to attack, which is almost like giving the opponent another defender. This is a common problem with younger players. Players should be in a good striking position on the field prepared to make a run at the proper speed and appropriate time so that the players arrive simultaneously with the ball.

Of course all the runs in the world won't do a team any good if its players cannot make the proper service, and practice time should be devoted to this skill as well.

· · ·

The interchangeable offensive style I prefer requires a great deal of movement from our players. First, however, the players must be taught about proper movement. Sometimes coaches stand on the touch line yelling, "Move! Move!" As a result the players are running around like crazy with no purpose, wasting a lot of energy because they're moving at the wrong time, to the wrong place and at the wrong speed. There's nothing wrong with players pacing themselves by standing, walking or jogging at times, but when a run is made it must be made with a purpose and at an accelerated speed.

Communication through eye contact is crucial to good offensive play. If a player makes a run but his teammate with the ball has his head down, the runner is wasting his time and effort. This is where one of the most basic fundamentals comes into play: keep your head up while dribbling.

When the dribbler's head comes up and eye contact is achieved, that's the time to make the run. A run not only creates an opportunity for the player making it, it takes defenders away from teammates and creates opportunities for them as well. A player indirectly can assist his teammates by being a "sacrificial" runner.

Some players are great at making runs and drawing defenders, then taking them into dead space to open up live space for teammates. Too many players want to make runs only for themselves, so they can receive the ball. Ultimately a great run does both, creating opportunities for the runner and his teammates.

Many times offenses bog down because players stand and want balls played to their feet while being closely marked, or their runs are straight up and down the field. It's a defender's joy to find a player who makes north and south runs. They're easy to track. A defender's nightmare is the player who makes an unpredictable run. It might start forward and then move laterally, or incorporate fakes.

Attacking players must learn to play their defenders into situations where they can beat them with a well-timed run. Too many offensive players let their defender mark them. A good attacker should always be thinking of how he can beat his defender, waiting for the moment when the defender looks away for a split second and then make a run to find open space.

This is where communication and chemistry come into play. Over time, and through practice, players learn to anticipate each other's moves and develop a sixth sense for where their teammates are going to be. This is another argument for full-sided match conditions during practice.

Certain attacking situations in different areas of the field lend themselves to various options. A team can have takeovers, overlap runs and one-two combination plays; it can send a third man through, it can set up near post and far post runs, and it can serve early crosses and late crosses. All of these attacking situations must be practiced to develop proper timing and recognition.

• • •

As stated before, communication is very important on offense, but much of it should be non-verbal. We often set up situations in practice where we don't allow the attacking players to talk, even in full-sided scrimmages. Players tend to get lazy and restrict their field of vision; they want to hear where their teammates are.

The problem here is the first call from a teammate might work, but the second one is going to tip off the defender for sure. Much of the talking players do while on offense is selfish talking — a player asking for the ball.

If a player finds space to receive a pass, the minute he opens his mouth he's informing the defender of his location. By being forced to remain silent during practice, the ballhandler assumes the responsibility for knowing the whereabouts of his teammates.

Coaches also can enforce the condition that players cannot call for the ball to be served to themselves. Allow the players to only give verbal direction for a player to pass to someone else. Many times three or four players are yelling at the ballhandler to pass them the ball.

Communication offensively should come from behind. If a wide back is in possession, his sweeper should be able to see the field and provide direction, rather than having a front runner call for the ball. The sweeper should be calling out direction such as "Wide to Mike!" to help the ball-handler, rather than yelling "Pass it back to me!"

When midfielders have the ball, the defenders behind them should be offering verbal instruction. They can see who's open. Too many times the communication is coming from the advanced players who are working hard to free themselves, and they spoil their effort by calling attention to themselves.

Hopefully by the time a team gets into an actual game, the communication process has been sorted out and the players know when to talk and what to say. Nothing frustrates and panics a player more than to hear several teammates yelling for the ball. This is something younger players in particular need to work on. Kids have a natural instinct to call for the ball.

• • •

If a coach is fortunate, he will have players from time to time who are blessed with exceptional attacking skills. He then must decide what limits, if any, to put on them. One extreme is to try to inhibit their style so they fit in with the rest of the team. The other extreme is to give them a totally free reign and let them do as they please, even at the expense of the team.

I believe one of the beautiful aspects of soccer is the individual flair players exhibit. It's thrilling when a truly gifted player gets the ball and the spectators know something exciting is going to happen.

Coaches should encourage more individual creativity. Coaches have traditionally emphasized getting rid of the ball, discouraging players from trying to create opportunities on their own. But if a player has exceptional skill, he shouldn't be harnessed too much.

In basketball, players such as Michael Jordan, Isiah Thomas and Magic Johnson can take over a game on their own. Every time they get the ball you're on the edge of your seat waiting for something to happen. I don't think it's a coincidence that all three of those players starred on teams that won at least two championships in the National Basketball Association in the 1980s. However, we have a shortage of players like that in soccer because we haven't encouraged that kind of individual flair.

This isn't to say team play should be ignored. Just as Thomas, Johnson and Jordan stayed within the framework of team play, so must soccer players. It's still a team game, so any individual play has to come within the team framework. If a player goes one-on-one every time he gets the ball, his team will suffer for it.

Players with a magical flair should be encouraged to use it, but only for the good of the team. Good players who have the ability and the flair to unbalance a defense should recognize when they've drawn two or three defenders and lay off the pass and let the other guy get the easy goal. They shouldn't do the work just for themselves.

Sometimes younger players who are standouts on their team — or believe they are — think they have to dribble everytime they receive the ball. They do their hard work for themselves, not for the benefit of the team. Developing the proper recognition of the game is an important part of a younger player's development. I've had some great dribblers who frustrated their teammates and in some ways stifled our attack because they didn't recognize when they should get rid of the ball. They didn't read the game.

A key factor in successful one-on-one encounters is that the offensive player must try to attack the defender head-on — not go around or away from him, but right at him. Speed is the attacker's best weapon. However, players must realize that they cannot always approach defenders at the same speed. They need to save an extra gear to accelerate by varying their speed.

Coaches cannot teach a player individual flair, however. Nobody ever sat down with Pelé or any of the other great ones and explained to them how to make the moves they made. They developed their own moves, sometimes on the spot. That was part of their genius. They practiced basic moves to develop better ball control and learn the fundamentals, but they acquired and perfected their own subtle moves.

What coaches can do is set up practice so that players are encouraged to develop their own moves. He can, for example, give awards or recognition for the best move to help create an atmosphere that encourages players to work on the individual aspects of their games. It's important to remember that a player doesn't need five or six moves; one effective move with a counter move is all that is really necessary. A lot of defenders have been familiar with the favorite moves of the great players, but that didn't mean they could stop them.

Small-sided scrimmages, from one-on-one to six-on-six, are effective methods of teaching players to enhance their individual skills. Smaller numbers should be used if there's a restriction, such as one-touch. A smaller playing area, such as $40 \times 40$, can be used, and it might be helpful to use more than one ball.

Coaches also can set conditions for attackers, such as requiring them to beat a defender before shooting. Have them create an opportunity with a dribbling move, or create an opportunity for a teammate by beating their man and then finding the open man. They should beat one defender, draw the second one, and then lay off a pass to a teammate.

Coaches also can set up exercises realistic to a game where two attackers go up against three defenders — two markers and one supporting player — and the attackers have to create opportunities through combination play and creative individual moves.

Many times coaches set up drills that give the numerical advantage to the attack, such as a three-on-two or two-on-one. Howver, it's more likely that attackers will face one-on-two, two-on-three or three-on-four situations. Coaches should structure their training to resemble more realistic game situations, where their attackers must be able to hold the ball and create opportunities on their own against a defensive numerical advantage.

• • •

Coaches also should emphasize a finish (a shot on goal) as often as possible in practice. This aspect of training is often ignored, as some coaches are content on working to improve dribbling and passing skills.

This also relates to why we haven't developed more soccer players in the United States with the magical scoring ability of a Pelé. We have not, in the United States, developed *goal scorers* compared to other soccer cultures. American players can control the ball and pass the ball, and are physically able to compete, but in the offensive third of the field they don't have the sophistication and the composure that players from other countries have. Too many American players lose their composure when they get in scoring position. They feel rushed, and rather than relishing the opportunity to score, they squander it.

Again, coaches can enhance the finishing ability of their players by placing them in scoring opportunities more often during practice. To not do so is like a basketball coach having his players pass the ball for 45 minutes during practice, and then have them take only three or four shots before heading for the showers. In basketball, kids have been shooting hoops since they were big enough to dribble a basketball. Soccer players, however, aren't likely to have a soccer goal in their backyard, so they are more likely to work on ballhandling skills.

The objective of soccer, however, is to score. That objective should be included, with full-sized goals and goalkeepers, in as many activities as possible. Almost *every* exercise, whether it is one-on-one or a full scrimmage, should include a finish as a major focus of the activity, not an afterthought. Ideally, a team has several goalkeepers, so that when it separates into smaller groups it still can include a shot on goal with each activity.

Through proper experience gained from practice, players are less likely to panic when they have a scoring opportunity in a game. This not only applies to forwards, but to all players. Too often a player tries to pass the responsibility off to someone else when he is in a good scoring position.

Goalkeepers also benefit when finishing situations are made game-like. They do not benefit as much when someone kicks still balls off the ground at them. The ball should be struck on goal while rolling, bouncing or while in the air. Coaches must always think back to the game and develop shooting exercises that resemble the situations that arise there.

Balls should be served to attacking players from behind, such as a midfielder giving a through ball to a forward, from crosses and from in front, as in a rebound or when a player delivers a pass from the end line. The serves should come on the ground and in the air.

Players can practice these situations without defense at first to improve their technique and speed, then opposition can be added to make it more functional.

• • •

Attitude also is a major factor in developing finishing skills. So many times, coaches stress passing and teamwork to the extent that shooting is downplayed. If a shot misses, the player receives negative reinforcement. Players must realize that not attempting to score is a greater mistake than missing a shot. They need to be encouraged to overcome fear of failure.

I believe a player who misses a shot on goal or loses the ball when attempting to beat someone at the proper time should be praised by his coach and teammates for a good effort. Players must be willing to take a risk at the appropriate times. A player cannot be discouraged by failure. The good forward might have the ball taken away from him nine times when he's trying to go to goal, but the 10th time he gets through. If he loses his confidence or worries about what his coach or teammates might say after failing a few times, he will have a very difficult time scoring.

It makes more sense to constructively criticize a player who fails to attempt an opportunity when it is available, whether it involves taking a shot or taking on a defender. Not to take the chance at all is far worse than taking it and failing. Of course the willingness to take risks should increase as a player nears the opponent's goal.

My philosophy is that the best players often make the most mistakes, basically because they're trying to accomplish positive things. In baseball, Reggie Jackson struck out 2,597 times, more than anyone in the history of the game. But people aren't likely to remember that. They probably remember that he hit 563 home runs. In soccer, a coach should allow his "home run hitters" to "strike out" on occasion. A player who comes to me after the game and says, "I had a perfect game; I didn't lose the ball once," doesn't impress me. That player might as well have been on the other team, because he probably played it much too safe. He made square passes or back passes, never took a run forward with the ball, and rarely put himself in position to fail.

I'm not advocating a "fools rush in" attitude, but I want players to be aggressive in their approach and take some risks. This involves the ability to make proper reads and early decisions with good vision, and that's one of the hardest things to develop. Players tend to want to watch the ball, receive the ball, control the ball, have some touches and *then* look up to see what to do.

The soccer players with great attacking skills know before they receive the ball what they're going to do with it. People said Pelé had eyes in the back of his head. Actually, his head was moving all the time when he didn't have the ball. He was like a banty rooster. When the ball came he had already taken all the pictures of the field and knew what needed to be done. He knew where his teammates were and where the defense was coming from.

This is one of the hardest elements to coach. When people refer to a player as being "skillful," many times they really mean that he has outstanding ball control. Skill also involves being able to use that ball control at the proper time and place by reading the game before receiving the ball.

What a coach *can* do is ask players to look up ahead of time and learn to read the game. We do that by playing one- touch in exercises, or perhaps two-touch or three-touch. If a coach asks the players what they least like to work on in practice, most of them would say one-touch or two-touch, because they have to use their brain. If they have to play one-touch, they're going to have to work hard at recognizing what's on before they receive the ball.

We have had several players with very good technique, and who were able to take full advantage of their skills by reading the game. But we also have had players who were not very intelligent from a soccer standpoint. They had a difficult time reading the game, and as a result made late decisions and improper decisions. Much of that is due to the fact they play within a very small field, so to speak. They play on a 10-yard field, rather than a 75 × 120 field. They see what's in their little area, but other than that they don't know what's going on. We have to broaden that focus, broaden their vision and make them more soccer intelligent. This is a challenge, but it can be done.

I remember one player in particular who was one of the most technically sound players I've ever coached, and also one of the best athletes I've ever had. However, he was not a skillful player because he just didn't see the field. He was able to beat people on his athletic ability and his good ball control. He was even able to play professionally for awhile. But his talent was like the tip of an iceberg. He never reached his potential because he did not improve his reading of the game and did not become a skillful player in the true sense.

It's frustrating for a coach to see talent like that wasted, both individually and for the benefit of the team. We tried everything we could, and improved his recognition some, but not as much as was needed. This is something many coaches don't spend enough time on, working with players in learning to read the game.

Video is very helpful in teaching players to have better vision. A coach can tell a player over and over again that he's not seeing the field, but if together they can review the player's performance on tape it helps get the point across. Maybe the player wasn't opening his hips to the field, or his vision was restricted to ball watching.

• • •

One of my favorite activities for developing offensive skills is a small-sided, three-on-three transition game. This exercise can accomplish many objectives, including the following:

- It exposes a player who does not work hard to get open. Many times when a player complains that he's not getting the ball enough it's his own fault because he's unable to find open space. No matter how good a player's offensive abilities are, if he cannot get himself into open space he is not going to be successful.
- It highlights players who know when and how to take on defenders.
- Using a 40-yard field with keepers and full-size goals, it shows which players can finish and which players need work on that part of their game.
- It shows which players are best at making immediate transition from defense to offense, and vice-versa, and exposes players who want to stand and watch when a change in possession occurs.
- It requires tight ball control and proper combination play in close quarters.

The three-on-three exercise can be utilized with various conditions. It can be done without forced marking, allowing the defenders to provide support, switch men or double-team. However, it also is effective when restricted one-on-one situations are enforced. Time should also be devoted to situations in which the defense has the numerical advantage to better simulate game conditions.

# 3

# Defense

To say that defense wins championships is a cliché, but it can be true. We allowed only one goal in our championship game in 1982, and allowed none in '83 and '88. We were able to control the ball a fair amount of time in these games, and at the same time we were able to stop our opponents when they were on the attack.

Defense has been the common thread of our program over the years. We haven't always had great attacking teams, but we've consistently played well defensively. That's because of the emphasis we place on defense and the attention we devote to it during practice.

In the early years of our program when soccer was a club sport, and then when it first became a varsity sport in 1973, we naturally didn't have an abundance of talented players. We were able to be competitive, though, because of our emphasis on defense. A great deal of our attack originated from our defense in those years. Although we have more attacking talent available today, we still take a great deal of pride in how well we defend.

I tell our players they're going to work harder on defense here than they ever have before. We find that some of the so-called "prima donna" players coming out of high school were given special liberties and aren't used to playing defense. They need a little attitude adjustment in regard to their work ethic and focus when the other team has possession of the ball.

However, these players soon learn that it's worth it. I believe the commitment we make to defense is one of the primary reasons a good number of our players have gone on to play professionally over the years. They've been able to compete with some of the more experienced international players because they are disciplined defensively. A sound defensive player can contribute to a team even if he doesn't have great offensive skills.

Good defensive play can be a great equalizer. It can make up for lack of offensive talent, to a degree, and it can cover for a team when the attack bogs down. Every team has the occasional game when it just can't buy a goal, days when its shots hit the goal post or it comes up against a hot goalkeeper. Excellent defense can pull a team through on these occasions.

•  •  •

Defense can be approached in different ways from a philosophical standpoint. This is most evident in World Cup play. The Germans utilize close man marking principles, which combines well with their aggressive attacking style. Other countries are geared more toward a zone defense. The Italians, for example, often fall back and get numbers up near their goal, and then generate offense through counterattack. Other countries play a defense that combines elements of both man-to-man and zone.

All defenses fall into the categories of a man-to-man marking system or a zone, or some combination of the two. Both systems have their advantages and disadvantages, and one could argue on behalf of either one.

The advantages of the man marking system include the following:

- Defenders can be matched up against an opponent's specific attacking strengths to neutralize their effectiveness.
- Individual defensive responsibilities are more easily defined and understood.
- An opponent's attacking weaknesses can be identified and exploited more easily.
- Specific problem areas are more recognizable and can be corrected more readily during a game.
- Time and space are more effectively eliminated from the opponent.

The disadvantages of the man marking system include the following:

- It is extremely demanding, both physically and mentally.
- It generally requires the use of a free back or sweeper, which is a specialized skill.
- Players executing a strict man-to-man system tend to be reluctant to go forward in attack out of fear of neglecting their defensive assignment.
- Providing support and depth can be more difficult, and players can become more isolated in their defensive roles. This leaves defenders facing an unfavorable matchup at greater risk.

A zone defense can be executed in one of several ways. Teams can play a high-pressure system that puts pressure on the ball, or fall back into a more conservative zone that places more players near their goal, with just one or two pressuring the ball.

Regardless of the approach, the advantages of a zone defense include the following:

- Players are responsible for areas of the field rather than specific players, which makes it easier to teach and more flexible.
- It is less physically and mentally demanding on each player.
- The defense can overload areas near its goal to make it more difficult for the opponent to score.
- It helps neutralize individual mismatches.
- The players generally feel as if they have more freedom to attack.
- It is easier for the defenses to stay more compact and not get stretched by the attacking team.

The disadvantages of the zone defense include:

- Attackers are allowed time and space when they move from one defensive zone to another.
- Communication can break down between defenders as attackers are switched from one zone to another, particularly if the defenders have not played together for a long period of time.
- Players tend to lose mental concentration, and are more prone to cheat at their work ethic because they are not individually exposed.
- It is more difficult to identify (and therefore correct) individual breakdowns.
- It can put players in a more passive frame of mind, which might affect their aggressiveness toward attacking.

• • •

At Indiana, one of our most emphasized defensive elements is to not play negatively by falling back and reacting to what the opponent wants to do. We strive to play aggressive, "positive" defense by trying to establish how our opponent will play and then working hard to stop it. Teams become frustrated if they are not allowed to do the things they are accustomed to doing offensively.

The greatest compliment a team can receive after a game is to have the opponent say, "We just didn't play our game today. It wasn't our day." That's another way of saying they were well-defended. Any opponent can play well if it is allowed to do what it wants to do. The idea is to take a team out of its favored style of play.

To do this requires a number of important factors. Three of the major defensive objectives are as follows:

- Recover ball possession as quickly as possible in a location closer to the opponent's goal than your own. This means your players must be more fit, more disciplined and more devoted to defense than the opponent.
- Allow the opponent only back, square or negative passes, not penetrating passes directed toward your goal. To do so, teams must apply tight pressure.
- Force opponents to take shots on goal from low percentage angles and distance after they reach the attacking third of the field.

I believe a man-to-man marking system accomplishes these defensive objectives more effectively. The primary problem I find with a zone defense is that it leaves the attacking team with too many opportunities to find openings as its players move from one defender's zone to another.

We do not, however, play a strict man marking system. In a strict man marking system, individual marking assignments are followed throughout the game. We use what I call the "most dangerous man" marking system. For example, we don't ask No. 3 on our team to always mark No. 9 on the opposing team. If No. 3 on our team goes up in attack and No. 9 on their team stays back, No. 3 would have to run all the way back to find No. 9 when we lose the ball. That's very demanding and often stifles a player's offensive contribution because he is too concerned about getting back on defense.

It is much better for players to be able to interchange defensive assignments so that they can get into the attack more quickly. Our defensive philosophy, therefore, is that when possession is lost, the players mark the most dangerous player on the other team closest to them. No. 3, who has been up in attack, would then find the most dangerous opponent closest to him at the instant the opposing team gains possession of the ball.

It is important for defenders to be patient and not leave their man to pick up a less dangerous opponent who has the ball. Defenders never should leave the man they are marking unless another opponent becomes more dangerous. The sweeper must provide good direction in order to maintain defensive balance and shape so that an unmarked opponent does not become a scoring threat. Disciplined man-to-man marking principles must be followed so that players do not get blind-sided or lose sight of opponents away from the ball.

A key that determines success both offensively and defensively is *recognition on transition and immediate communication and adjustment*. We work very hard on this.

For example, if No. 3 is close to two players from the opposing team, he must quickly decide which man to mark and communicate his decision to his teammates. That's where the sweeper must contribute in sorting out the marking. He is the coach on the field, and must constantly be communicating with his teammates. The goalkeeper must help in this regard, too. Their teammates, in turn, must be willing to listen.

This system demands that all players be able to defend well. The front players and midfielders will at times find themselves marking attacking players, so it is crucial that they develop sound defensive techniques to go with their offensive skills. Defenders generally will be in the same vicinity as their opposing attackers, but they also will need to interchange from front to back and laterally.

Occasionally teams might face an opponent with a player who is such a great scoring threat that the coach assigns one player to defend that player exclusively. He sacrifices his player's offensive contribution in this case, therefore such a move should be done only in extreme circumstances. The defender would shadow his man all over the field, and not leave him even when his team has the ball. This strategy does not mean the other players can relax on defense.

Sometimes coaches allow their most gifted offensive players to rest when the other team has the ball. They don't require them to mentally or physically devote themselves to defense because they're saving themselves for attack. I don't believe, however, that a team can have a prima donna forward resting on defense. That places an added burden on the other players. If everybody shares the load and maintains the philosophy that they are defending as a team, each player has an important defensive role to play.

This philosophy has been one of the major reasons for our success over the years. We've worked very hard on the individual and team principles of defense, and we insist that everyone share the load and work hard for each other.

An offshoot of this philosophy is that it builds better team unity. If coaches allow certain "glamour" players to relax on defense and avoid the dirty work, other players are likely to resent it, and that can have a negative effect on the team's performance. If everyone shares responsibilities and opportunities, it helps create a better overall team atmosphere.

• • •

Although the ultimate objective of the defending team is to regain possession of the ball, it is important not to lose sight of another important priority: stopping the opponent from scoring. Regardless of a team's specific approach, certain defensive principles apply in achieving this dual objective.

## Pressurizing

The act of limiting the space and time an attacker has to play the ball, pressurizing should begin the instant ball possession is lost. It is at this very moment many players lose concentration and are most vulnerable to attack.

Pressurizing distance should be as close as possible, ideally one to two yards. Players also should be goalside of the ball so that an attacker cannot make penetrating, positive passes or attempt a clear shot on goal.

Inexperienced players tend to pressurize more loosely because they are afraid of getting beat. This is a vital mistake, because it gives the attacking player time and space to pick his options, whether it be to dribble, pass or shoot.

At Indiana, we attempt to force our opponents' scoring opportunities to come from at least 20 yards. Teams obviously have a better chance to stop shots from longer distances and from poor angles. It is wise to monitor the types of shots opponents are generating. This is done easily through videotaping and charting each scoring opportunity.

## Support and depth

Defenses restrict the space between defenders and behind defenders away from the ball through the process of support and depth. Proper supporting depth and angles must be taught; they vary depending on the speed and ability of the attacker, the location of the ball, the position on the field and the location of the other defenders.

Generally, the supporting defender away from the ball should be no more than five yards from his opponent. He should be as close as two yards when the attacker reaches shooting distance. The definition of "shooting distance" depends on the ability of the attacker, but it generally is the edge of the penalty area. The proper angle for the supporting defender is generally 45 degrees, but this also depends on the body position of the pressurizing defender.

The supporting player must also pass on proper information to the pressurizing player, such as whether he should commit to the tackle and which direction he should attempt to jockey the ballhandler.

## Compactness

Defenses must stay compact and avoid being stretched too far, both front to back and side to side. Teams that do not remain compact allow too much space to the opposing team, and it becomes very difficult to properly pressurize and provide support.

## Communication

Proper communication is vital to good defensive play. The supporting players must communicate with their teammates to let them know where they are and to instruct them on what they might not be able to see.

The sweeper and goalkeeper must be the primary communicators because of their positions on the field, but all players must take responsibility in the communication process that weaves a defense together. Players should be encouraged to talk during practice to develop the habit, although there is nothing like actual game competition to hone a team's communication skills.

My 1979 team that had 18 shutouts in 22 games probably communicated with each other better than any team I've coached. That team had seven seniors, and they had played together for a few years. Veteran players tend to have a better understanding of each other and the game, and tend to be more confident. As a result, they usually are better communicators.

Communication also helps establish mental discipline and control on defense, and helps keep panic from setting in. Players are less likely to let down if teammates are offering them support and encouragement.

## Delay and cover

When a team loses possession of the ball, players must get goalside of the ball quickly to blunt the opponent's attack. During this process, pressurizing players try to delay the attack by jockeying and shepherding ballhandlers into less dangerous areas of the field, such as the touch line, so that all defenders can get into proper supporting positions and avoid a numerical disadvantage.

Patience on the part of the defender pressurizing the ballhandler is necessary in this situation. If he overcommits on a tackling attempt and fails, he places the rest of the defenders in jeopardy.

Players on the "weak" side, or away from, the ball should take the quickest recovery route to the danger area and then determine their best strategy. It might be to challenge for the ball, delay the player with the ball, mark another attacker or provide support.

This process should involve the entire team, not just the backs. Teams that effectively drop back in an intelligent and well-executed manner not only delay the attack by marking the attacker's forwards, they improve their chance of frustrating the attacking team and regaining possession of the ball.

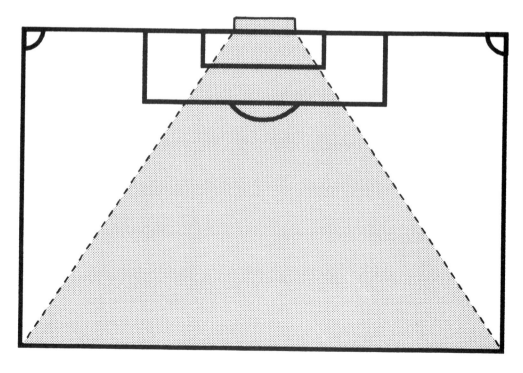

This process is largely a matter of hustle. By getting back into a proper position quickly, the defense can prevent the attacking team from gaining the numerical advantage it seeks. It comes down to knowing where to go and getting there quickly.

As a team retreats, it should do so in a funneling pattern toward goal (see illustration on page 66), therefore concentrating the defenders toward the middle of the field. The concentration should become more compact as it nears the goal.

## Tracking

This is particularly important in a man marking system. Defenders must be able to track opponents who are not in possession of the ball, while keeping the ball in view at all times. They cannot put themselves in a blind side position by being a ball watcher and losing track of the attacker they are marking. This is an important skill and requires discipline and concentration as well as proper positioning.

Defenders should be able to see the ball and their man at all times. They should position themselves to intercept a pass that might come to their man, make a tackle as their man receives the ball, or prevent their man from turning the ball toward goal.

• • •

Most of the teams at higher levels of competition play with two marking backs and a sweeper, therefore front players must defend against an extra player. At times they will have to work very hard. They can't defend all three opponents man-to-man, of course, so teams must use combination man-to-man and zone marking.

If, for example, the opponent's right back has the ball, one of the forwards should be marking him while the other forward covers their two other backs. Teams want to encourage the opponent to make square passes, so the far side (away from the ball) forward should be withdrawn in case the opponent's backs should decide to come forward.

As a general principle, leave the far side — the weak side — of the field open. If the ball is in the center, controlled by the opponent's two central defenders, the forward withdraws and does not go forward to pressure the sweeper; that would leave open a pass to a marking back. The outside forwards must stay with the wing backs in this situation. If the opponent attacks with wing backs, a team's forwards must work extra hard to nullify the opponent's attack.

If the opponent uses its backs in attack, an option is to use one of the forwards as a chaser to keep pressure on the ball, and perhaps force the opponent's backs to one side of the field. The other forward tries to limit the passing opportunities between the opponent's other backs.

Another option is to send a midfielder forward to defend so that the opposing backs are all marked and have the other midfielders play a zone defense. This strategy gives the opponent a man advantage in the midfield. This is a good strategy to use when the opponent generates its attack out of the back and does not like to build through midfield. A third option would be to play without a sweeper by having the sweeper push up on their center striker and have everyone else mark up the opponent closest to him. If the opponent is very strong coming out of the back and a team wants to disturb the attacking rhythm, this strategy can accomplish that and change the momentum of the match.

• • •

Special attention must be given to weak side defense in practice. The biggest danger for an opposite-side defender is to be caught ball-watching and get blind-sided by players running behind him. Too many players lose concentration and become ball-watchers. They need to discipline themselves to watch the ball and still not lose sight of the man they are defending.

As a general principle, when the opposing team has possession on the right touch line, defenders must mark opponents tightly who are near the ball. The weak side defenders play more loosely, but not so loose that they can't intercept a pass when the point of attack is switched, or make a tackle when the ball is served in that direction.

• • •

Forced man marking exercises quickly reveal players who cheat defensively, because nobody can cover for them. We use forced marking as a teaching tool, such as in a three-on-three situation. We'll go with two- or three-minute bouts of hard transition work.

Teams should not neglect one-on-one defensive principles in training. At times it is wise to apply a restriction, such as no tackling. Too often, younger players want to commit and win the ball from an opponent when that is the last thing they should be thinking. An opponent with the ball has the advantage, and the defense must find ways to take that advantage away.

One-on-one exercises should be done between goals up to 30-40 yards apart, with goalies, and should end with an attempted shot on goal. Too many times these activities are done without a finish and the players forget about attempting to score. This has kept players in the United States a bit behind the rest of the world. Players should be conscious of scoring goals at all times.

•  •  •

One of the biggest weaknesses we find with new players joining the team concerns tackling. We work very hard on commitment. Unless a player is 100 percent sure of winning the ball, we don't want him to tackle. The good attackers are just waiting for a defender to attempt a tackle, to stick a leg out. Then they're gone.

Front players, of course, have a little more freedom in this regard, but players in the defensive half of the field cannot take chances. They need to be patient and show restraint when confronting an attacker in possession of the ball.

We want our players to pressure the dribblers without committing and wait for doubleteam help from behind, or shepherd the ballhandler away from the danger zones. The minute a defender commits to a tackle and fails, the team is playing at a numerical disadvantage.

It's also difficult to teach players not to go for foot fakes when an attacker fakes a shot or pass. A lot of times defenders have their eyes focused on the opponent and not the ball, and we have to work hard defensively to get our players to react only to the ball.

Learning how to properly run backward also is an often-overlooked, yet important technique in defense, as is knowing how to turn properly using the shortest radius. If a player needs to improve his ability to run backward, we'll have him practice marking a moving attacker. The exercise progresses into a more match-related setting by adding extra players and two goals.

• • •

We don't use the offside trap defensively, because it takes a great deal of understanding and communication. The professional teams that play together day after day and year after year can do it, but it's not practical for college teams or younger teams. Even if a team executes the trap perfectly, all it takes is for one linesperson not to catch it. Most teams that utilize the offside trap a great deal get burned, either by poor communication or by poor officiating.

# Restarts

**R**estarts, or set plays from free kicks, corner kicks and throw-ins, are often overlooked when determining soccer strategy. Yet it has been estimated that nearly 40 percent of all goals are scored directly or indirectly from set plays. The more evenly matched the teams are in a game, the more likely it is that execution of set plays will determine the outcome of the game.

Our national championship in 1982 was largely the result of executing restarts. Our first goal in a 2-1 eight-overtime victory came when Gregg Thompson scored off of a throw-in. Our second goal came off of a free kick by Thompson.

Set plays present excellent scoring opportunities when executed in the attacking third of the field for several reasons, including the following:

- Specific plays can be rehearsed many times during practice to maximize timing and each player's technical abilities.
- Several attacking players, as many as nine, can be involved in the play in a concentrated area.
- The defenders must be at least 10 yards from the ball on free kicks and corner kicks, leaving the kicker with an unobstructed opportunity to accurately serve the ball.
- The play always is initiated with a still ball, which helps ensure accuracy.

Coaches should resist the temptation to install multiple play combinations for restarts. It is better to be able to execute a few plays extremely well than it is to have many plays that have not been mastered. Even if the opponent knows what a team plans to do on a restart, it is difficult to stop if it executes well.

Set plays pose a challenge for coaches during practice. They are time-consuming and they involve little activity, so the players are standing around for a substantial period·of time. Players can become bored and lose concentration.

We have our restart specialists work on their own before or after practice each day, and then work on restarts with all the field players involved for 10-15 minutes at the end of practice. We also practice restarts within a full-sided scrimmage occasionally by calling fouls that did not occur to practice free kicks, or setting up corner kicks as we see fit. We also might work on corner kicks at the end of practice, taking 10 from each side of the field against a full defense.

## Throw-ins

The throw-in is the most common of all restarts — each team takes up to 60 each game — and for that reason alone it merits special attention from a strategic standpoint. It can be much more than a simple method of putting the ball into play when well executed.

Defensive players often relax and lose concentration when throw-ins are taken, probably because the play often appears inconsequential. This provides an excellent opportunity for an attacking team that has a well- practiced strategy.

The most fundamental strategy for the attacking team regarding throw-ins is to make the play quickly. Defensive players who are tired or simply lack concentration are likely to be resting during this break, and they can be exploited. Therefore, the player closest to the ball should make the throw whenever possible. An exception would occur when the team's best long thrower is needed to initiate the play in the attacking third of the field.

The throws generally should be made to whichever player happens to be unmarked, because that player can best advance the ball and start the attack. This requires quick thought and action on the part of the thrower, as well as his teammates.

If at all possible, the throw should be made forward toward the opposing team's goal. This forces defenses to make recovery runs, and creates a potential scoring opportunity. If no opening exists in that direction, however, the ball should be thrown back to an unmarked player. That player can then look to move the ball forward.

The player making the throw should recognize that he is making a pass, just as he does on the field of play, but with his hands instead of his feet. The ball should be thrown into an area and at a pace that enables the receiving player to make a constructive play. If the receiving player is to head the ball back to the thrower, for example, the ball should be thrown at the receiving player's chest, which would allow him to head through the top half of the ball back to the thrower's feet.

The thrower also should make it a point to become part of the offense as soon as he inbounds the ball, rather than standing on the touch line and watching. He can try to support the player with the ball and create a numerical advantage in that area, or make a run to draw the defense and create an opportunity for a teammate.

The receiving players should be careful not to set up too close to the thrower, or to each other. By spreading out, they create more offensive opportunities and make it more difficult for the defenders to mark them.

The strategy for throw-ins also depends on the part of the field from which the throw-in is made and the strength of the thrower. Teams throwing from the defensive third of the field should play it safe; retaining possession is the most important thing. The ball should not be thrown to the center of the field unless a teammate is wide open. If possession is lost, it can set up an immediate scoring opportunity for the opposing team.

Teams throwing from the middle of the field can afford to take slightly greater risks in moving the ball forward, although they still must emphasize retaining possession. Tactics such as switching and dummy runs are an effective means of setting up a positive attacking play. Players running to receive the ball should make sharp runs and cuts to create openings.

In the offensive third of the field, teams can take greater risks in trying to set up a scoring play. Throw-ins from this area of the field are similar to free kicks and corner kicks.

The ball can be thrown near the goal to create a quick scoring opportunity, perhaps even a one-touch strike. In this area of the field, getting the ball in quickly to catch the defense off guard takes on greater importance. The player nearest the ball should make the throw, and look for a penetrating pass. Teams cannot be offside on throw-ins, so a pass beyond the defense to an attacking player running toward the goal can be particularly effective.

Substantial practice time should be devoted to throw-ins, particularly from the attacking third. A team's strongest and most accurate throwers should be identified during practice so it is clear who should make the throws during games, when possible. The most effective throws are low, flat and hard, so that the receiving player can play the ball more effectively.

If a team is in the attacking third of the field, and it has a player capable of throwing the ball into the six-yard area, a long throw can set up an immediate scoring opportunity. The ball should be thrown with a low trajectory to the near post area. Ideally, a tall player will be in that area to head the ball into the goal or slip a pass to a teammate. Other teammates should make sharp runs to the goal area to play balls that get through to their attacking space. The timing of the support runs is crucial in making this play a success.

• • •

The most important factor in defending throw-ins is to get prepared quickly. Alert attacking teams will play the ball quickly, so the defense must not use this time to rest.

Overall, the basic principles of defense apply to throw-ins. It is important to mark all possible receivers, and then pressure the ball after it is thrown. Someone also must mark the thrower, so that he cannot run inbounds and receive a return pass without defensive pressure.

Teams at higher levels have players capable of throwing the ball into the six-yard area. These instances require special defensive attention. The defenders should shut off as much space as possible in the penalty area. They can position players in front of or behind the player receiving the throw, if not both, and position the goalkeeper in the front half of the goal.

# Direct free kicks

Direct free kicks offer excellent scoring opportunities when taken from inside the 'D' (the arc at the top of the penalty area) or from favorable angles. They should not be taken lightly.

When taking kicks from this area, the attacking team can be sure that the defenders will form a wall to protect a portion of the goal from the driven shot. The goalkeeper, meanwhile, will stand off to one side so that he can see the ball's flight and protect the part of the goal not blocked by the players forming the wall.

Attacking strategy, therefore, should focus on screening the goalkeeper's view of the ball to make it more difficult for him to save the shot, whether it is driven or chipped.

The most common and effective method of accomplishing this is to place players from the attacking team near the defenders' wall, thereby blocking the goalkeeper's view. These two or three players should be placed less than 10 yards from the ball, two or three yards closer to the kicker than the defending players. This prevents them from being offside, and enables them to obscure more of the goal then they could at a greater distance. It also makes them available to score off of rebounds.

The attackers should stand close together, with their feet closed, so that the goalkeeper does not have a "window" to look through. They also should break after the ball has been kicked; however, if they leave too early, they allow the goalkeeper to pick up the ball's flight more easily. They should converge on the goal from opposite sides in case they have an opportunity to play a rebound.

We like to assign the people who take our free kicks rather than have whoever is closest to the ball make the kick. When we get in position to score on a free kick, we want to take full advantage of the opportunity by having specialists kick the ball. Unless a team has someone who can serve the ball with proper pace and accuracy, chances of success are diminished. Teams are just kicking a ball into the mixer and hoping for the best otherwise.

It is common strategy to have two or three players line up to make the kick. This helps place the defensive players off-balance. They don't know which player will kick the ball, and the player who does not make the kick helps screen the goalkeeper's view.

The two potential kickers should approach the ball from opposite angles at a brisk pace. Ideally, one of the players would be right- footed and the other left-footed. They will have decided before approaching the ball who should kick the ball and what type of kick should be made. The player not making the kick should run slightly in front of the ball to further block the goalkeeper's view, and should continue toward the goal to play a possible rebound. The first player to reach the ball can make the kick, too, however.

Three basic shots are available to the kicker:

- A drive through the attacker's portion of the wall
- A bending shot around the outside of the wall
- A bending shot over the wall

The sharper the angle from which the kick is taken, the fewer options available to the attacking team. It generally is best to play the ball to the back of the defense — preferably to the near post, and preferably with a bending kick. To accomplish this, a kick from the right side of the field should be taken by a left-footed player, and a kick from the left side of the field should be taken by a right-footed player.

With free kicks around midfield, where we don't have a realistic scoring opportunity, we like to put the ball into play as quickly as possible to try to catch the defense unaware, just as in the case of throw-ins.

● ● ●

Defending against free kicks near or inside the penalty area requires a team to set up a wall. This is a necessary evil of set play defense in the attacking third of the field; without it, the attacking team would have a clear shot at the goal. However, it places the defense at an extreme numerical disadvantage. Because of this, it is essential that all defensive players execute their jobs properly.

One player must be designated to set up the wall. It can be a goalkeeper or a field player. In either case, this must be worked out in practice to avoid confusion during games. At Indiana, we use a field player.

If a field player is in charge of lining up the wall, he should stand out field approximately 10 yards from the wall and in line with the goal post with which the wall is to be set. If the kick is taken from a wide angle, the wall should be set on the outside of the near post to make a driven shot more difficult. If the kick is taken from a more central position, the wall should be set up according to the goalkeeper's preferences, which should be established during practice.

The only player that needs to be positioned is the player on the outside of the wall. He should be in a direct line between the ball and the post, 10 yards from the ball. The rest of the players forming the wall line up next to him.

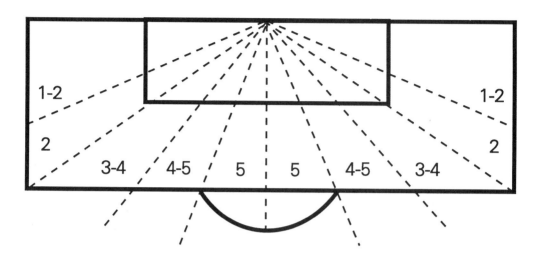

The number of players used to form the wall depends on where the kick is made from (see chart above). Generally, the more central the position of the kick, the more players needed in the wall. If the kick is made from the 'D', as many as five players should be used to form the wall. If the kick is made between the 'D' and the corner of the penalty area, three to five players should be used. If the kick is made from near the side of the penalty area, one or two players should be used.

The closer to the touch lines or to the defending third of the field the kick is taken from, the fewer the number of players required to form the wall. In some instances, only one might be needed.

Teams should be prepared so that they know how many players to use in forming a wall under any circumstance. The goalkeeper, or another player, can shout the number to help maintain order. Players need to know ahead of time who will be used for the wall, and where they should stand. Ideally, a team's best defenders should not be in the wall; they will be needed to mark attacking players after the ball is put into play. At the same time, the wall must have courageous players willing to take a hard-kicked ball to the body.

The players should stand close together, with their feet less than a foot apart, so that the ball cannot be kicked between them or through their legs. The tallest player should stand on the outside of the wall, and the shortest on the inside. In instances where three or more players are forming the wall, one player should stand outside the player lined up with the near post to defend against bending shots around the wall. The goalkeeper usually takes a position on the far post side of the goal line.

Occasionally players forming the wall link arms or put their arms around each other's waists. This is not recommended, because the players are not able to protect themselves from the force of the kick, and their movement after the kick is restricted.

The players forming the wall should protect themselves as much as possible by crossing their hands in front of their lower abdomen and groin area and lowering their heads slightly so that ball does not hit them directly in the face. At the same time they must stand tall and not leave their feet or turn their backs to a hard-driven shot.

The players should break from their positions *after* the ball is kicked. It is better to break too late than too early, because an early break could create an opening for the kicker. It generally is best for the players in the wall to move together toward the ball after it is kicked, to increase their chances of blocking a subsequent shot on goal.

The placement of the defensive players away from the wall also is vitally important. All of them should be used; the scoring opportunity for the attacking team is too great not to take advantage of all available resources.

The position of these players depends on the placement of the ball before it is kicked. When the kick is made from inside the 'D', the defense must guard the area of the field between the six-yard area and the penalty area.

## Indirect free kicks

Indirect free kicks, when taken within the 'D', are similar to free kicks taken from the same area. The difference is that the kicker cannot take a direct shot on goal; he must play it to a teammate first. Therefore, a slight adjustment must be made in the placement of the attacking wall.

Indirect kicks from inside the penalty area are rare, but teams must be prepared for them. The defense probably will place all 11 players inside the goal area, or on the goal line if the kick is taken within 10 yards of the goal.

If the ball is positioned at a sharp angle from the goal, the first touch should be made with the purpose of widening the angle. If necessary, the ball should be played backward, to improve the angle and provide more

time for the shot on goal. The shot should be taken to an area opposite the position of the goalkeeper.

Indirect kicks taken outside the attacking third of the field should be taken as quickly as possible to take advantage of any lack of organization on the part of the defense. At least two players should move toward the ball quickly to enhance the speed and effectiveness of the play. Meanwhile, the players in advance of the ball should get behind their opponent.

Choreographed patterns are not needed in the non-attacking two-thirds of the field. Here, attacking teams should focus on getting the ball into play quickly and taking advantage of whatever openings the defense allows. The best approach is to use some degree of improvisation.

• • •

Defending indirect free kicks is much like defending direct kicks near the penalty area. The defense must be aware, however, that a direct shot toward the goal is unlikely unless the attacking team is hoping for a deflection into the goal, such as off the body or head of a player in the wall. More likely, a pass will be made first to change the angle of the shot.

The defense must try to cover as much of the goal as possible with a wall. In some cases, if the ball is placed close to the goal, all 11 players will be standing on the goal line within the goal posts. In these instances, the goalkeeper should stand in the middle of the wall.

After the first kick is taken, but before the second touch, the wall should converge on the ball. This better enables those players to prevent the shot and provides an opportunity to catch the attacking players offside.

## Corner kicks

Corner kicks provide excellent scoring opportunities, particularly when two or more players combine to create a shot on goal, such as with a header. Most teams get about 10 corner kicks during a game, and each one offers a terrific scoring opportunity.

A team's strategy on corner kicks should depend on the individual strengths of its players. An accurate kicker is essential, of course. He must be able to serve the ball to an unmarked area of the goal, at an exact spot where it can be played by a teammate. Inswinging bending balls present the most difficulty to the defending team.

Teams that lack such a kicker — youth teams in particular — have other options available to them. They can take advantage of the 10- yard rule and make a short pass from the corner. The receiving player can then try to create a play, and often will have a two-on-one or three-on-two numerical advantage to try to exploit. More advanced teams should be prepared to make scoring attempts directly from the inbounding kick.

Generally, at least one player will be positioned on the far side of the goal, just outside the penalty area. This player, or players, should be one of the team's most skilled headers. He will make an angled run and attempt to meet the kicker's pass for a shot on goal, or nod the ball back to the near post for a teammate to shoot on goal.

Another player should be close to the far post, just outside the six-yard box. He is in position to make a short run toward goal, but also can go back to play a pass. Also, someone should be placed in the mid-goal area, and someone on the near post area of the goal from where the kick is made.

Most successful plays are made to the near post area, but not by a wide margin over other areas. Corner kicks to the near post area are more likely to be accurate because of the shorter distance, and they create many options for the receiving player. He can try to flick the ball into the goal with a one-touch maneuver, or play it to a teammate for a shot on goal. He also can come off the near post and take a short corner pass, then try to create a play by dribbling or passing.

A few corner kicks to the near post can be an effective means of setting up scoring opportunities in other areas. Because of the difficulty in defending the near post, defenses often concentrate on that area — which can leave an opening at mid-goal or at the far post.

Despite the various strategies available on corner kicks, attacking teams should leave themselves room for improvisation based on how the defense sets up. Players who are not designated to play in specific positions near the goal should line up according to what the defense leaves open, filling in where they will have the best opportunity to participate in the play. Blind-side runs are an effective means of creating scoring opportunities on corner kicks.

• • •

Because of the options available to the attacking team, defending corner kicks is a difficult task. The most important principles are to get enough bodies near the goal to give the defense a fair chance to stop the play, and to not get caught watching the ball.

The best setup ordinarily is to put all the midfielders and one or two forwards near the goal. It usually is best to leave one player near the halfway line in case a fastbreak opportunity arises. All players in attacking positions should be marked, and the goalkeeper should be provided plenty of support at the near and far posts.

Defense at the near post is particularly crucial, as many teams play the ball into that area. The defenders there must be prepared to cut off a bending serve and a hard low drive, to mark attackers in that area and to watch out for angled runs.

The position of the goalkeeper depends on what he perceives to be the tendencies of the attacking team, based on scouting. In years past it was common for the goalkeeper to play in the area of the far post, but as more teams focus on making corner kicks to the near post, the goalkeeper must adjust by playing at mid-goal or closer.

Communication is of the utmost importance for goalkeepers after the corner kick is made. He must make a clear, positive call to let his teammates know his intentions and avoid excess confusion in a situation that is chaotic by nature. Corner kicks often demand that the goalkeeper punch the ball out of the goal area, rather than trying to catch it.

Just as the attacking team must improvise according to the defensive play on corner kicks, the defenders must be prepared to adjust according to the alignment of the attacking team. The posts must be protected, but the rest of the goal area coverage must be flexible, depending on the what the offense does.

A cardinal rule for defenders on corner kicks is to play the ball aggressively. It does no good to have everyone in proper position if the defenders allow the attacking team to play the ball unchallenged. Because of the intense assault on its goal, it is natural for the defense to be in a somewhat passive state of mind, reluctant to make a play for the ball out of fear of leaving the goal unprotected. Defenders near the goal must challenge for the ball as aggressively as the attacking players.

# 5

# Fitness Training

**T**he importance of fitness training in soccer should be readily apparent. No other team sport demands as much in terms of cardiovascular endurance and muscular strength. Yet many players and coaches fail to devote enough time and energy to achieving maximum physical condition.

Even the most skilled players are useless to their teams if they aren't in peak condition. Many times, the team that wins the close game in the final minutes is the one that is in the best physical condition. Fitness training also builds mental toughness and discipline that can carry over to game performance; likewise, lack of conditioning can lead to fatigue, which causes a loss of concentration and detracts from performance.

Today, the top players must be able to perform to the best of their abilities for at least 90 minutes. The "one-way" player no longer has a place. When in possession of the ball, every player must concentrate fully on attack. When the opposition has possession, every player must devote himself totally to defense.

We won our first national championship in a game that lasted eight overtimes. Our second championship was won in a game that went two overtimes. We obviously wouldn't have been able to win those titles if we had not been in excellent condition. Regardless of the level of competition, players are bound to participate in close games in which conditioning plays a major role in determining the winner.

Basic fitness training needs that must be met are as follows:

1. **Running endurance.** Soccer players must be able to run almost continuously for 90 minutes, at varying speeds.

2. **Speed.** Players must have that extra "gear" to accelerate past opponents.

3. **Strength.** Players need to be able to kick harder, throw farther, tackle more powerfully and jump higher than their opponents. Strength also helps prevent many injuries common to soccer.

4. **Muscular endurance.** Players must be able to use their strength over a long period of time while jumping, heading, dribbling, shooting, tackling, twisting, turning and changing direction continuously.

5. **Flexibility.** Players must have a complete range of motion to better execute their skills. Flexibility also helps avoid some injuries.

At the major college level, it is essential that the players devote ample time to fitness training during the off-season. Coaches simply cannot afford to spend a great deal of practice time on conditioning. Members of youth league teams, of course, cannot realistically be expected to follow an off-season fitness training program. High school players can, perhaps, to a lesser degree.

Regardless, if the players aren't already in shape, fitness training must become a major focus of practice. It should be approached gradually, however, so that players do not suffer injuries resulting from over-exertion.

Many coaches tend to shy away from fitness training because it's no fun, for them or the players. They want to improve their players' skills and they want their players to like them, so they are reluctant to devote much time to the "dirty work." That's a mistake, at least at the higher levels of play. However, fitness training can be incorporated into many training activities that also improve ball skills.

Players of all field positions require the same conditioning program, although goalkeepers merit a slight exception. Goalkeepers need to have endurance, but not in the same way as a player who has to run for 90 minutes. They require a more explosive type of conditioning, which can be achieved through activities such as taking a rapid succession of shots on goal for a designated period of time. There's no magical length of time, but 30-40 seconds is common.

When I played high school and college soccer in the late 1950s and early 1960s, we did a lot of running without the ball to improve our fitness. My teams now do very little conditioning without the ball during the season. It is more efficient to incorporate running with specific skill activities.

Some coaches believe players must actually run sprints to achieve complete aerobic conditioning. The line of thinking here is that players cannot run as fast with the ball as they can without it, therefore they do not achieve the full conditioning benefit from practice activities. This is true, but running at full speed can be incorporated into practice in other ways. We get in a lot of sprinting while working on transition between offense and defense, for example. I don't believe you need to run up and down the field without a specific purpose.

During the off-season, however, players should follow a structured running program so that they report to practice in peak condition. The off-season running program our players use follows. It is designed to prepare them for the start of practice in mid-August, but it can be adapted to fit any team's schedule.

# Off-Season Fitness Training Program

| MONDAY | TUESDAY | WEDNESDAY |
|---|---|---|
| Stretch | Stretch | Stretch |
| Jog 1/2 mile | Jog 3 miles until July 15 | Jog 3/4 mile |
| Stride to sprint 100 yards, 18 repetitions (30-second rest between each sprint) | 660-yard sprint | Jog 4 miles between July 16-31 |
| | Jog 5 miles between August 1-12 | Jog 1/4 mile |
| Stride to sprint, 40 yards, 15 repetitions (15-second rest between each sprint) | Five 40-yard strides (30-second rest between each) | 550-yard sprint |
| | | Jog 1/4 mile |
| Jog 1/2 mile | Five 40-yard backward strides (30-second rest between each) | 220-yard sprint |
| Restretch | | Jog 1/4 mile |
| | Restretch or scrimmage | 110-yard sprint |
| | Jog 1 1/2 mile | Jog 200 yards |
| | | 40-yard sprint |
| | | Jog 1/2 mile |
| | | Restretch |

| THURSDAY | FRIDAY | SATURDAY |
|---|---|---|
| Stretch | Stretch | Stretch |
| Jog 3 miles until July 15 | Jog 1/2 mile | Jog 20-30 minutes |
| Run 80 yards, walk 20 yards (10 repetitions with no rest) | Restretch | |
| | Walk 1/4 mile | |
| Jog 5 miles between August 1-12 | Run 40 yards, walk 15 yards (15 repetitions with no rest) | **SUNDAY** |
| Five 40-yard strides (30-second rest between each) | Backward sprints on level surface (50 yards backward, walk back to start; 8 repetitions) | Rest! |
| Five 40-yard backward strides (30-second rest between each) | Jog 1 1/2 miles | |
| Restretch or scrimmage | | |
| Jog 1 1/2 mile | | |

• • •

A soccer player's sprinting ability is an important asset to his performance. Many occasions will arise during a game in which a player needs to get from one point to another at top speed. Therefore, improving one's speed can improve one's game.

To improve speed, concentrate on the following fitness components:

1. Increase stride length through flexibility and sprint drills.
2. Increase rate and efficiency of arm and leg movement. One must also relax and utilize best angles of motion.
3. Improve starting ability, both from a standing and crouched stance.
4. Increase endurance. This enables one to maintain rate of speed through sustained stride length.
5. Improve flexibility to utilize a full range of motion in the hips, lower back, shoulders and ankles.
6. Increase strength through hill running and weight training. Additional strength enhances explosive leg power and speed through greater stride length.

While running sprints, athletes should concentrate on lengthening the stride as much as possible without over-striding, and keeping the stride low to the ground without bounding. It also is important to run erect, staying up on the toes and holding the chest high.

At the same time, athletes should run as relaxed as possible. This enables them to move their arms and legs with maximum efficiency and speed, and minimizes fatigue.

Sprinting, of course, also enhances conditioning and stamina. Allow only enough rest between sprints to maintain proper form for each effort.

Sprints are most effective when performed over a distance of no more than 60 yards. This distance enables the athlete to maintain an emphasis on form and effort. It is best for the athlete to accelerate in a steady, relaxed manner for 20 yards, sprint for 20 to 50 yards, and then gradually decelerate for 20 yards.

The following exercises can be incorporated into speed work:

**High knee.** Run forward, lifting the knee until the thigh is parallel to the ground. When the right leg is lifted, the left leg should be pushing off the ground in a forward direction. The emphasis should be on form, and the drill should not be hurried. It is important to maintain correct upright body posture. The high knee lift action is sustained during the 20-yard action phase of the drill.

**Plantar push.** Emphasis is placed on speed and a strong plantar push. The down extended leg and foot is checked for a full response off the running surface as the opposite knee is fully lifted as rapidly as possible throughout the 20-yard action area

**Leg reach.** Lift the knee high, followed by a full extension of the foreleg. This action is an attempt to reach the maximum stride length. It is necessary to focus on balance, as the knee is fully lifted and the lower leg is thrust forward into the reaching position.

The arms also should reach forward (staying low) with each leg reach action. The arm that is back should not go behind the hip. Again, quality of form is emphasized, as speed is not as important as achieving a high knee lift and full extension of each lead leg.

**Quick lift and reach.** Utilize high knee action and leg reach action as rapidly as possible while maintaining proper form. More emphasis is placed on speed so that there is a greater carryover to race situations.

**Relaxation.** The focus of the high knee and leg reach action in this drill is on complete body relaxation. The jaw and facial muscles should be totally relaxed, and the arms and hands must be loose, but under control. This relaxation enables maximum speed of movement with a minimum loss of expended energy.

These exercises should be performed in sets of four, in the following order:

1. 4 sets of high knees
2. 4 sets of fast leg plantar push
3. 4 sets of leg reach
4. 4 sets of fast lift and reach
5. 4 sets of relaxation

• • •

Weight training has become more acceptable in recent years as a means of supplementing all sporting activities, including soccer. Some coaches have their players continue a full weight training program throughout the season, but we do not. Our players might lift some to maintain their strength during the season, and players who are particularly weak in one or two areas of the body will concentrate on those. But the primary part of our weight training program is done during the off-season.

Players should be working hard in their regular practice sessions, and they need to be fresh for the games. To lift weights in addition to their regular practice sessions might be too draining. Players should achieve peak condition during the off-season and then maintain most of that during the season.

Still, muscular strength is as important as aerobic fitness in performing at a peak level. Strength training stimulates circulation, helps maintain flexibility, increases appetite and neuromuscular control and enhances the sense of well-being.

The fundamental principles of a strength program should be as follows:

- Each exercise should work as much of the body as possible.
- Free weights should be used along with resistance machines.
- Consistency must be maintained. Strength training cannot be ignored for any long stretch of time. It should be part of a player's off-season workout schedule at least three days a week, on alternate days.

The time and energy invested in training, during the season and otherwise, should be maximized to its fullest. Athletes have neither the time nor energy to waste on ineffective or insufficient training methods.

A warm-up period should be an integral part of any workout schedule. Muscles cannot approach their maximum capability unless they are first properly loosened up by performing similar, less rigorous movements. An athlete cannot warm up properly for bench presses, for example, by performing standing presses. He must perform a set or more of bench presses with a resistance well below the maximum he can lift first.

A set is a series of repetitions. A repetition is one complete execution of an exercise. Studies indicate that muscular strength is best increased by performing five to eight repetitions per set. No more than three sets should be necessary for any exercise.

Before lifting, jog about one-half mile, then stretch. After completing the weight program, stretch again before performing any prescribed running or ball work.

A rest period of no more than two minutes should be taken between sets. All sets of a particular exercise should be performed in succession before beginning the next exercise.

## Weight training tips

- Always warm up properly before lifting. This should include stretching for 10-15 minutes and jogging at least one-half mile.
- Proper technique is a must. Never sacrifice technique for added weight. Improper technique can lead to strength loss and injury.
- Be consistent. Progress will come only if an athlete works out regularly in a disciplined fashion.
- Progress systematically. An athlete should increase the weight by no more than 10 pounds after he is able to comfortably complete a set of the prescribed number of repetitions.

The following off-season strength program can be adapted to any team's schedule. Each phase should last three to four weeks. Younger players should not perform any exercise program without first consulting a doctor and a fitness expert.

A nearly endless variety of weight training exercises are available that can help improve a soccer player's performance. A sample routine and a description of the major exercises follows.

| MAJOR LIFTS | Phase 1 (sets/reps) | Phase 2 | Phase 3 |
|---|---|---|---|
| Bench press | 4 × 10 | 4-5 × 6<br>2 × 6<br>2 × 4 | 1 × 10 |
| Squats | 4 × 10 | 4-5 × 6<br>2 × 8<br>2 × 5 | 1 × 10 |
| Power cleans | 4-5 × 6 | 4-5 × 4-5 | 4-8 × 2-4 |
| Step-ups | 4 × 8-10 | 5 × 5-6 | 4 × 8-12 |
| AUXILIARY LIFTS | | | |
| Leg curls | 3 × 12 | 4 × 8-10 | 3 × 15 |
| Upright rows | 3 × 12 | 4 × 6-8 | 4 × 10 |
| Side lunges | 3 × 8 | 3 × 6 | 3 × 10-12 |
| Leg extensions | 3 × 12 | 4 × 8-10 | 3 × 15 |
| Straight arm pulldowns | 3 × 10 | 3 × 8 | 3 × 12 |
| Toe raises | 3 × 15 | 3 × 15 | 3 × 20 |
| Manual neck resistance | 2 × 10 | 2 × 10 | 3 × 10 |
| Abdominal crunches | 3 × 20 | 3 × 25 | 3 × 30 |

# Bench press

**Benefit:** Overall development of the chest

**Equipment:** Bench and barbell, or bench press station

**Procedure:** Lie on your back on a flat bench with your legs positioned at each side of the bench with your feet flat on the floor. Grasp the bar with an overhand grip that is about six inches wider than shoulder width, then raise it to arms' length. Slowly lower the bar until it touches the middle of your chest. Inhale as you lower the bar. After the bar gently touches your chest, slowly lift it back to arms' length as you exhale.

Your buttocks and shoulders should remain on the bench at all times, and you should have only a slight arch in your lower back as you execute this exercise.

**Caution:** The bench press is dangerous because the bar can fall on you if it slips from your hands or if you cannot support the weight. You should have a spotter nearby, particularly when lifting weights close to your maximum capability, or use a safety rack, which enables you to crawl out from under the bar if it falls.

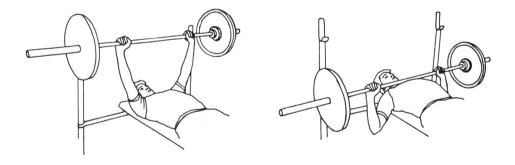

# Squat

**Benefit:** Development of the lower back, hips and buttocks

**Equipment:** Barbell and squat rack

**Procedure:** Step under the bar on the rack and place it on your shoulders, stabilizing it with a comfortable grip. Keep your chin up, your back straight and your feet shoulder-width apart, with your toes pointed slightly outward. Inhale as you slowly lower your body until your thighs are parallel with the floor. Make your movement smoothly; do not bounce at any point. Keep your knees out over your toes. Stand up in a powerful motion, exhaling in the process. For added safety, you may squat over a flat bench, touching it with your buttocks at the bottom of your motion.

**Caution:** Be careful to use the proper technique to avoid possible injuries to your back or knees. Do not attempt this exercise with more weight than you are sure you can handle to avoid the risk of falling or dropping the bar. Do not bend lower than the prescribed position.

# Leg curl

**Benefit:** Development of the hamstrings

**Equipment:** Leg curl station

**Procedure:** This exercise can be performed with weights attached to your feet, but it is much easier to execute with a machine designed for the purpose. Lie face down with your lower legs extending over the edge of the bench (your knees should be just off the pad) and the back of your ankles under the pads or weights. Hold on to the front of the machine or bench for support. Keeping your hips on the pad, slowly raise your lower leg as high as possible, touching the back of your buttocks if you can. Return slowly to the starting position.

**Caution:** This is a safe exercise. Be careful, however, not to lift your hips off the bench as you lift, and do not position yourself so that your legs hyperextend when in the starting position.

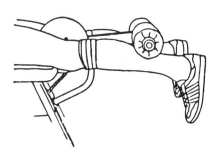

# Toe raise

**Benefit:** Development of the calf muscles

**Equipment:** Raised platform and barbell, or machine station

**Procedure:** This exercise can be performed with a barbell and something to step onto, or at a machine designed for this purpose. Place the barbell on your shoulders, or step underneath the weights of the machine. Stand on the balls of your feet; your heels should not be touching the platform. Raise up on your toes as high as possible. Pause and slowly lower. Pointing your toes straight ahead works the main calf muscles. Pointing your toes outward works the inner calf muscles. Pointing your toes inward works the outer calf muscles.

**Caution:** This is a safe exercise. Be careful not to bounce as you lower the weight, and keep your knees straight.

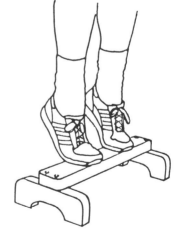

# Upright row

**Benefit:** Development of the upper back and shoulders

**Equipment:** Barbell or upright cable rowing station

**Procedure:** This exercise can be performed with a barbell, or on a machine with an upright rowing station. Grasp the barbell or handles with your palms facing inward and your hands about hip width apart. Stand erect with your arms extended downward. Pull the weight straight up almost to your chin, keeping it as close to your body as possible. Keep the elbows up and out as you reach the top of the movement. Pause and slowly lower the weight to the starting position.

**Caution:** This is a safe exercise. The only danger comes from dropping the barbell, or attempting to lift too much weight and injuring the back.

# Side lunge

**Benefit:** Development of the thighs

**Equipment:** Barbell

**Procedure:** Place the barbell on your shoulders along the upper back. Your feet should be positioned close together, your chin up and your back straight. Inhale and step out at a 45-degree angle with one leg until your thigh is nearly parallel to the ground. Keep your stationary leg straight, bending the knee as little as possible. Exhale and step back to the starting position. Repeat the movement with the other leg. Alternate back and forth.

**Caution:** It is important to perform this exercise with proper technique. Perform the movements smoothly to avoid excess stress on the knees and back. Do not bounce at the end of the lunge, and do not dip too low.

# Leg extension

**Benefit:** Development of the quadriceps and knees

**Equipment:** Leg extension machine

**Procedure:** This machine can be performed with weight attached to the feet, but it is better to use a machine designed for the purpose. Sit on a bench with the top of your ankles touching the pads, or with the weights attached. Position yourself so that the edge of the bench is against the backside of your knees. Hold on to the seat next to the hips. Keep your toes pulled upward toward your knees, exhale and raise the weight until your legs are fully extended. Pause, inhale and lower the weight slowly and under control to the starting position. Keep your upper body still during the exercise.

**Caution:** This exercise is safe. Be careful not to bounce the weight or hyperextend the knees after lifting.

# Straight arm pulldown

**Benefit:** Development of the triceps

**Equipment:** High pulley or lat machine

**Procedure:** Grip the bar or handles about three feet apart, if possible. Step back from the machine so that your arms are extended in front of your head and are supporting the weights. Bend forward slightly at the waist, keep your elbows slightly bent and locked, inhale and pull the bar straight down to the top of your thighs. Keep your elbows locked throughout the movement. Return to the starting position and exhale.

**Caution:** This is a safe exercise. Be careful to stand correctly to avoid possible injury to the back.

# Neck resistance

**Benefit:** Development of the neck muscles

**Equipment:** Neck machine station, or none

**Procedure:** This exercise can be performed at a machine designed for the purpose, or with nothing but your hands and arms. To perform it without a machine, sit on a flat bench with your back straight. Place both hands on your forehead and lay your head back as far as you can with your chin up. Resisting with your arms, push your head forward until your chin touches your chest. Make the movement on a six count. Reverse the movement with your hands on the back of your head, pushing your head backward. Also place your right palm against the right side of your head and resist, then switch hands and resist to your left side.

**Caution:** This is a safe exercise, particularly when performed without a machine. Be careful not to make a jerking motion with the neck, and do not attempt to push too much weight when using a machine.

# Power clean

**Benefit:** Development of the hips, legs, lower back and buttocks

**Equipment:** Barbell

**Procedure:** Place the barbell on the ground and stand over it. Bend your knees to grab the bar, keeping your back straight, and focus your eyes on a line slightly above the floor. Straighten your knees, shrug your shoulders and pull with your arms, swinging the bar out in front of you and up until it is "racked" on your chest.

**Caution:** This is an advanced lift, and should only be attempted with the supervision of an experienced coach or trainer. The dangers include the possibility of back injuries, losing your balance and having the bar land on top of you or spraining a wrist.

• • •

Stretching is an important part of fitness training that should not be overlooked. It used to be that players warmed up by performing ballistic stretching exercises and calisthenics, such as jumping jacks. Today the format is more sophisticated. We use an active stretching program that requires about 15 minutes each training session. It helps reduce many of the injuries that are common to soccer, such as groin pulls, and increases the players' flexibility.

Flexibility means a muscle can move through its *entire range of motion* easily and efficiently. Flexibility is somewhat determined by genetics; some athletes are naturally limber, while others are "stiff." All athletes can enhance their flexibility, however, through proper stretching.

Stretching your muscles achieves the following:

- Reduces the viscosity of muscular fluids
- Mobilizes blood reserves
- Generates heat in the muscle due to metabolism of contraction and relaxation, which enables the muscle to contract more powerfully
- Improves range of motion, which enhances nourishment of the joints

The end result is that the athlete will have greater dexterity, be better able to utilize his strength, and reduce his chances of injury.

An athlete should never force a stretch by bouncing on the muscle. This can cause an injury to the muscle, ligaments or cartilage. When a muscle is stretched too far, the body signals for a rapid contraction of the opposing muscle group (which is called a stretch reflex) and an injury can result. Usually an application of heat will relax the muscles and permit stretching, as will a basic warm- up routine such as jogging or light exercise.

When stretching, move the body or limb segment through its range of motion until you feel discomfort, but not pain. Maintain this position for 30 seconds, then release and repeat, each time trying to go a little closer to the full range. The stretching must occur gradually. It also helps to try contracting the opposite muscle group you are trying to stretch. For example, when stretching the hamstrings, contract the quadriceps.

To achieve maximum results, the athlete must start conditioning the muscles before the season begins. Proper training will substantially reduce muscle injuries, which generally occur when muscle fibers are stretched beyond their capability. A muscle that is unprepared for abnormal motion won't be able to withstand elongation.

• • •

The number of stretching exercises available is limited only by the number of muscles in the body and your imagination. Some basic exercises follow:

1. **Single knee to chest.** Bend your leg and pull your right knee to the chest, touching it to your forehead. Hold for 30 seconds, straighten leg, repeat for left leg.

2. **Straight leg pull.** Lay on your back and grasp the toes of your right foot with your right hand. Straighten your leg until your hip comes off the ground. Hold for 30 seconds. Repeat with left leg.

3. **Groin stretch.** From a sitting position, place the soles of your feet together and pull your heels as close to the buttocks as possible. With your hands on your ankles and elbows on your knees, push down with your elbows to try to get your legs flat on the ground. Hold for 30 seconds. Repeat.

4. **Ballerina.** Stand with your heels touching together and toes pointed outward. Bend over and touch the ground. Hold for 30 seconds without bouncing. Repeat.

5. **Hurdler's stretch.** Sit on the ground with your left leg stretched straight forward and your right leg bent so that the sole of the foot touches the inside of the left leg at the knee joint. Place your left hand on the floor or the ground at the left side. Reach forward with your right hand to touch your left toe. Hold for 30 seconds. Change leg positions and repeat.

6. **Stride stretch.** Stand on your left leg with the right leg extended parallel to the floor or ground. Place your hands on your hips then reach forward with both hands and try to touch the right foot. Hold for 30 seconds. Repeat with the opposite leg forward.

7. **Cross the tee.** Lay on your back with your arms perpendicular to your body. Swing your right leg high upward to touch your left hand. Hold for 30 seconds, then repeat on the opposite side.

8. **Straddle toe touch.** Sit with your legs outstretched at an angle. Lean forward and touch both feet with your hands (right hand to right foot, left hand to left foot). Hold for 30 seconds. Repeat.

**Single knee to chest**

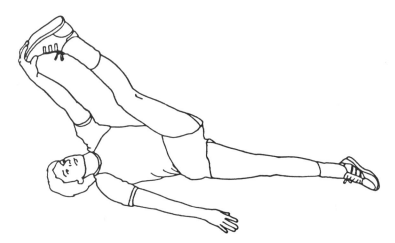

**Straight leg pull**

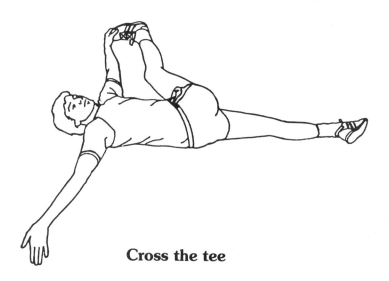

**Cross the tee**

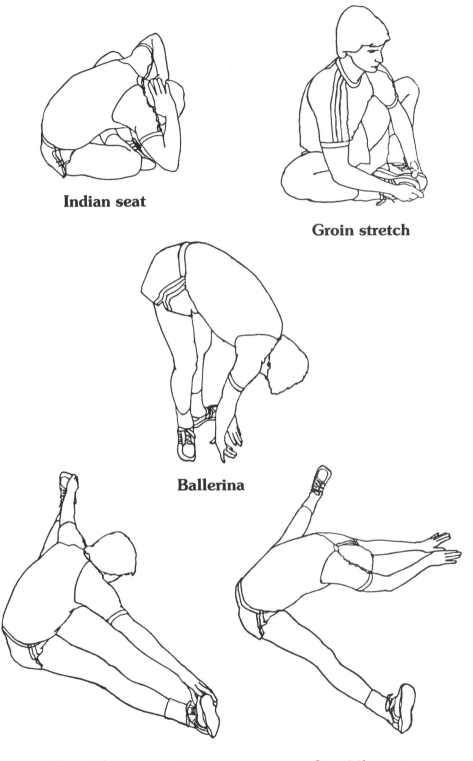

**Indian seat**

**Groin stretch**

**Ballerina**

**Straddle toe touch**

**Straddle seat**

9. **Straddle seat.** Spread your legs as far as possible and lean straight ahead, trying to touch your chest to the ground. Hold for 30 seconds. Repeat.

10. **Indian seat.** Sit on the floor or ground with your legs crossed at the ankles, Indian style. Put your hands behind your head with your elbows back, then lean forward and try to touch your forehead to your ankles. Do not put pressure on your head with your hands. Hold for 30 seconds. Repeat.

• • •

At Indiana University, we test our players' fitness and performance level three times a year to monitor their progress — upon their return to campus at the start of pre-season practice, upon the completion of the season and at the end of the academic year following the second semester training program.

Over the years, we have established norms and standards of performance. Players then can see how they compare to others, and hopefully are motivated to improve their performance level.

The testing items we use are as follows:

1. Two-mile run
2. Forty-yard dash
3. Bent leg sit-ups for one minute
4. Chin-ups
5. Standing broad jump
6. Vertical jump and reach
7. Obstacle dribbling
8. Kick for distance (stationary ball, with both feet)
9. Throw-in for distance
10. Head for distance
11. Kicking accuracy

• • •

Rest is as important to physical fitness as activity. Intensive processes of nutrition, food absorption and recovery of structural proteins and high-energy compounds take place in the organism during rest following intense activity.

The greater the intensity of the activity, the more extreme are the processes of recovery. If exercise is regularly repeated, body changes become firmly established and lead to growth of the working organs and to structural and functional perfection.

A normal training session should include breaks, as part of the recovery process takes place during these periods. Athletes should fill these intervals with a different kind of activity to speed recovery.

The fundamental part of the recovery process, however, takes place at night during sleep. Changes occur in the nerve cells of the core of the brain during this time, reducing the excitability of the centers which house various senses: hearing, sight, touch, and so on. Sleep calms the brain cells, replenishing their work capacity for the forthcoming activity of the organism.

Insufficient sleep causes the cells to become overloaded and leads to exhaustion. The amount of sleep required to replenish the body varies with each individual, but eight hours is adequate for most people.

• • •

Mental fitness is nearly as important to reaching your potential as a soccer player as physical fitness. Each player should develop a positive attitude toward his teammates, his coaches, the opponents, the laws of the game, the officials who enforce those laws, and most important, himself.

Only positive, constructive comments should be allowed between players. Negative comments and gestures quickly destroy player relationships and lead to the deterioration of team morale. Likewise, only positive comments should be directed toward an official by a player. Giving the proper respect to the laws of the game and the officials pays dividends in the long run. If a team cannot win within the framework of the rules, then victory is worthless.

Opponents are to be respected, and any intentional physical or verbal abuse should not be permitted. A rabid "kill the enemy" approach is counterproductive, because players need to address their full attention to their individual roles. At the same time, if a player becomes intimidated by the opposition, he loses concentration and becomes a much less effective team member.

Each player must feel good about himself and see himself as a worthy team member. He must be willing to work hard to prepare in order to achieve.

Following are some questions each player should be asked, or should ask himself, when trying out for a team.

1. What is your objective in soccer?
2. Are you willing to pay the price to find out how good you can be?
3. Are you willing to follow good personal habits relating to health and safety?
4. Are you willing to keep fit during the off-season?
5. Are you willing to work with your teammates toward a common goal?

If you have the desire to be the best and are willing to work toward excellence, you have the right attitude to be a part of a successful soccer program. The potential of your team depends directly on the potential of each player.

If *every* player trains and performs to the best of his ability, the team will be at its best. This is the ultimate anyone can hope for. Be proud. Don't settle for less than your best. This is the challenge. Are you willing and ready to accept it?

# About the Author

Jerry Yeagley entered his 30th season as soccer coach at Indiana University in 1992. Since 1973, when the sport was granted varsity status, the Hoosiers have won more than 300 games. Yeagley's teams won national championships in 1982, '83 and '88, have advanced to the Final Four nine times and have appeared in the NCAA tournament 16 times. As a player, Yeagley was a member of the Myerstown (Pa.) High School state championship team and the West Chester State (Pa.) NCAA championship team.

Yeagley is a two-time winner of the NCAA Division I Coach of the Year award, a recipient of the prestigious Bill Jeffery Award for his unique contributions to college soccer, a member of the Pennsylvania Athletic Hall of Fame in Carlisle, Pa. and a member of the National Soccer Hall of Fame in Oneonta, N.Y.

# MASTERS PRESS

DEAR VALUED CUSTOMER,

Masters Press is dedicated to bringing you timely and authoritative books for your personal and professional library. As a leading publisher of sports and fitness books, our goal is to provide you with easily accessible information on topics that interest you written by the most qualified authors. You can assist us in this endeavor by checking the box next to your particular areas of interest.

We appreciate your comments and will use the information to provide you with an expanded and more comprehensive selection of titles.

Thank you very much for taking the time to provide us with this helpful information.

Cordially,
Masters Press

Areas of interest in which you'd like to see Masters Press publish books:

☐ COACHING BOOKS
    Which sports? What level of competition?

☐ INSTRUCTIONAL/DRILL BOOKS
    Which sports? What level of competition?

☐ FITNESS/EXERCISE BOOKS
    ☐ Strength—Weight Training
    ☐ Body Building
    ☐ Other

☐ REFERENCE BOOKS
    what kinds?

☐ BOOKS ON OTHER
    Games, Hobbies
    or Activities

Are you more likely to read a book or watch a video-tape to get the sports information you are looking for?

I'm interested in the following sports as a participant:

I'm interested in the following sports as an observer:

Please feel free to offer any comments or suggestions to help us shape our publishing plan for the future.

Name _____ Age _____

Address _____

City _____ State _____ Zip _____

Daytime phone number _____

# BUSINESS REPLY MAIL

FIRST CLASS MAIL    PERMIT NO. 1317    INDIANAPOLIS IN

POSTAGE WILL BE PAID BY ADDRESSEE

MASTERS PRESS

2647 WATERFRONT PKY EAST DR DEPT WF

INDIANAPOLIS IN 46209-1418